INDIAN BANNERSTONES
& Related Artifacts

IDENTIFICATION AND VALUE GUIDE

Lar Hothem
&
James R. Bennett

COLLECTOR BOOKS
A Division of Schroeder Publishing Co., Inc.

Front cover: Top, left to right: Double crescent bannerstone, Aaron & David Kilander collection. Grooved atl-atl weight, Jon Dickinson collection. Middle left to right: Reel bannerstone, Jon Dickinson collection. Notched butterfly bannerstone, Dennis Link collection. Bottom left to right: Claystone bannerstone, John McCurdy collection. Ball bannerstone, Jon Dickinson collection. Rose quartz bottle bannerstone, John Dickinson collection.

Back cover: Top to bottom: Atl-atl hook, Museum of Native American Artifacts. Slate geniculate, Jon Dickinson collection. Tallied tube bannerstone, Dennis Link collection.

Cover design by Beth Summers
Book design by Beth Ray

COLLECTOR BOOKS
P.O. Box 3009
Paducah, Kentucky 42002-3009

www.collectorbooks.com

Copyright © 2009 Lar Hothem and James R. Bennett

The current values in this book should be used only as a guide. They are not intended to set prices, which vary from one section of the country to another. Auction prices as well as dealer prices vary greatly and are affected by condition as well as demand. Neither the authors nor the publisher assumes responsibility for any losses that might be incurred as a result of consulting this guide.

Searching for a Publisher?

We are always looking for people knowledgeable within their fields. If you feel that there is a real need for a book on your collectible subject and have a large comprehensive collection, contact Collector Books.

Proudly printed and bound in the
United States of America

Contents

Dedictation 4

Acknowledgments..................................4

About the Authors 5

Assisting a Fellow Author...................6

Introduction 7

Atl-atls, Weights & Bannerstones.......................8

A Look at Bannerstones 13

    Winged Banners 13

    Double Bit Axe Banners...........................21

    Ball Banners 22

    Tube Banners 26

    Pick Banners...............................34

    Geniculates 39

    Panel Banners..............................42

    Other Style Banners 44

Utilitarian or Ceremonial? 65

Tie-on Atl-Atl Weights........................74

Boatstones &Bar Amulets 93

Miniature Bannerstones.....................95

Salvaged Bannerstones 96

Manufacture & Preforms 105

Atl-Atl Hooks & Handles 146

Valuation Factors 153

Building a Bannerstone Collection.................155

Museum Quality Bannerstones 170

Dedication

To Sue Hothem, who has become a dear friend, and who has shown me that while unwanted changes do happen in life, they can be overcome. I can think of no one else Lar would have wanted this book dedicated to more than Sue.

Acknowledgments

When I first took on this project, I had a basic knowledge of the works of some of the early noted authors who addressed bannerstones in one capacity or another such as Knoblock, Moorehead, and Webb. While their writing was instructive and at times thought provoking (especially with regard to some of the theories put forth by Dr. Webb), I found myself thankful that a more recent author took the time, energy, and dedication to author a truly first class publication in all respects on the topic of bannerstones: that author being Mr. David L. Lutz, author of *The Archaic Bannerstone — Its Chronological History and Purpose from 6000 B.C. to 1000 A.D.* published in 2000. While other references of various sizes and mediums have been published over the years on the topic of bannerstones, I consider Mr. Lutz's book a truly monumental accomplishment, and one that provided me with a greater understanding of the chronological sequence that bannerstones underwent in their 5,000 year history.

When I took over this project, I was handed a cardboard box stuffed full of notes, clippings, envelopes and letters, and hundreds of 35mm photos with small notes attached to them. Most all of those photos were of artifacts brought to Lar by collectors who had visited him in order to make their cherished artifacts available to him for study and photography. I wish to thank all who traveled to meet with Lar and offered him their assistance with this project. I would also like to offer my personal thanks to Larry Garvin of Back to Earth Rocks & Relics, a close personal friend of Lar, for his assistance with helping to see that this project continued, and for introducing Sue Hothem to me as a potential co-author.

While many people contributed photos and opened their collections to me for study as well as photography, I wish to offer those who allowed me the pleasure of visiting in their homes and studying the vast collections they had assembled my sincerest appreciation for some wonderful evenings. My thanks go to Mr. John McCurdy, Mr. Charlie Wagers, Mr. Eric Wagner, Mr. Jon Dickinson, Mr. Tom Davis, Gene and Tim Edwards, Mr. Charles Ray, David and Aaron Kilander, and Mr. Cliff Jackson. Thank you all for allowing me to inspect, handle, and photograph some of the finest bannerstones currently housed in private collections. I appreciate the hospitality I received from all the aforementioned gentlemen.

A few names I have been proud to mention in my previous books as friends as well as consultants are those of my fellow Ohio collectors Bob Bright, Charlie Fulk, and Doug Hooks. As I delved into this project, once again they made themselves available to help me find answers to my many questions. The times we sat around the kitchen table drinking coffee and reviewing photographs and artifacts for this book are some of my fondest memories of my participation in this project.

Jim Bennett

About the Authors

Lar Hothem

Jim Bennett

Lar Hothem
July 26, 1938 – October 18, 2006

While most collectors of Indian artifacts have read or known of books written by the late Lar Hothem, the true extent of his writing may be bigger than some realize. Lar was a lifelong Ohioan, and enjoyed collecting around the counties in central Ohio where he resided.

While owning several small businesses, Lar authored more than 700 articles on many topics appearing in over 75 regional, national, and special interest publications. Lar was a long-time contributing editor to the *Antiques Journal*, wrote the "Arrowheads" chapter of the Time-Life Collectibles Series, and was a frequent contributor to the *Columbus Dispatch Sunday Magazine.*

Lar's life-long interest in collecting, studying, and writing about North American prehistoric Indian artifacts began at a young age on the Hothem family farms. Beginning in 1976 he launched into a successful career as an author, becoming one of the country's most respected authorities on collecting North American Indian artifacts.

His numerous identification and price guide books (over 35) have proven to be indispensable to both beginning and advanced artifact collectors as well the amateur archaeologist. Lar wrote regularly for *Indian Artifact Magazine, Prehistoric Antiquities Quarterly,* and the *Ohio Archaeologist.*

Lar was an active member of The Standing Stone Chapter and the Kokosing Chapter of the Ohio Archaeological Society, several other local and state archaeological societies, the Ohio Historical Society, and the Ohio Genealogical Society and Fairfield County Chapter of the Ohio Genealogical Society.

Jim Bennett

Another life-long Ohioan and avid artifact collector, Jim Bennett resides in rural Ashland Co., Ohio, in the north central part of the state, and began his collecting by walking fields and buying artifacts from his Amish neighbors. While Jim enjoys working on his farm and being a father to his four children, his love for collecting ancient relics has taken him over a 20 year journey that has lead him to his current career of running an artifact website, catalog business, auction house, and his true passion, the writing artifact-related books. Jim has authored five books on the subject of ancient Indian artifacts with an emphasis on the identification of authentic vs. reproduction artifacts.

Jim is the founder and a board member of the Authentic Artifacts Collectors Association, an internet-based association of collectors and dealers, over 4,000 members strong, dedicated to the collecting of authentic artifacts. Jim also sits on the board of the directors for the Museum of Native American Artifacts in Bentonville, Arkansas.

Twenty years ago, while crossing a field while hunting, I stumbled across my first arrowhead, purely by chance. Like most people who enter this collecting field by finding a random artifact, I immediately had questions about that which I had just found. How old is this item? Who made it? What is it worth? These questions tend to lead most people straight to the local library in search of answers, and I was no different. Within a few hours of finding that first flint point that was to be the beginning of a life-long passion for artifacts, I found myself pacing the aisles of our county library looking over various titles of books I thought might help me find the answers I was looking for. It didn't take long for me to come across a book on arrowheads written by a gentleman named Lar Hothem. I returned home and spent the evening paging through Mr. Hothem's book, amazed as I learned how old arrowheads really were, how many different types could be found, and totally mesmerized by the thought of holding something made so long ago in the palm of my hand. As I opened that book and began reading the first chapter, a new chapter to my life was also beginning, though I knew it not at that moment.

Since that day, over 20 years ago, I came to know Mr. Hothem's books quite well. Being a fellow Ohioan, I also had the opportunity to meet and speak with Mr. Hothem on a regular basis at various shows and events throughout the next couple of decades. Like everyone else who had the pleasure of knowing Lar, I came to know him as a gentle and soft spoken man who truly loved the hobby of artifact collecting, and there was no doubt that he possessed a true passion for writing about this hobby which he so enjoyed.

Though I wish I could say that Lar and I became close friends over the years, I cannot. Rather, like so many other collectors, I knew Lar mostly though his writing, and the occasional brief conversations held over the stacks of books that filled his tables at relics shows as I perused his selection of new and used titles.

When I began writing my first book (*Relics & Reproductions*), I called and spoke with Lar who was quick to answer my questions regarding publishing, and he later assisted me by adding my books to the Hothem House inventory.

A short while after Lar's untimely passing, I came in contact with Sue Hothem, Lar's wife. Mrs. Hothem and I began corresponding, and our conversations brought us to a discussion of this book on bannerstones which Lar had begun, but was not able to finish. Sue had stated that this book was one which Lar had always wanted to do, and he was very excited about the work he was completing on it, and she greatly desired to see this work completed. Hence, my involvement with this project was established, and work was begun to complete this final book by Lar Hothem.

As Lar's writing helped me to get started in the hobby of artifact collecting, and his assistance with my first book helped me to get a start as an author, it has been my honor and my pleasure to be able to repay him for his assistance by helping with the completion of this book.

Jim Bennett

Introduction

The purpose of this book is not to introduce the reader to a plethora of profound new theories or evidence with regard to bannerstones and their use in ancient times, nor is it to present an in-depth study in support of cultural affiliations and timeline chronology with respect to the atl-atl weapon system. Rather, the purpose of this book is to share with fellow collectors interested in bannerstones and other artifacts relating to the atl-atl some wonderful examples that are currently housed in private collections around the country, and to help collectors gain a perspective of their approximate associated values. While I have attempted to outline some of the issues that continue to keep bannerstones in the problematical artifact classification, I have refrained from citing personal speculations as to their possible ceremonial nature as too much remains unknown at this time about such matters, other than the fact that there does appear to be a link between some styles of bannerstones and some unknown ancient ceremonial or mortuary practice.

When I first viewed the outline Lar had penned for this project, it was evident that the direction he wished this book to take was to provide a look at not only bannerstones, but also other atl-atl component parts as well as ceremonial bannerstone styles which most likely were never used in association with a working atl-atl weapon. I have done my best to stick with Lar's original outline, and I have used as many of the photographs taken by Lar as was possible throughout this book.

While bannerstones are known to be a component part to the atl-atl, having been excavated in direct association with other atl-atl components, many designs do lead one to speculate if their use may have actually been purely ceremonial in nature. Other stone artifacts more utilitarian in design were also manufactured for use with this weapon such as loaf stones, bar weights, and other more nondescript tie-on styles of weights, and thus, these types have also been included in this book. In addition to these stone counter balance components, I have also included some examples of atl-atl hooks and handles to help give the reader a full understanding of all of the component parts of the atl-atl weapon.

When first reviewing Lar's outline and some written instructions he had penned to whoever was to finish this book, Lar had noted that he was undecided if certain gorgets and other flat slate styles as well as the various forms of birdstones should be included in this book as their presence in certain excavations leads one to believe a possible association with the atl-atl may exist. As I worked through Lar's outline, I also pondered the question of whether or not to include certain style gorgets he had photographed for this book. After several months of thinking over the outline and direction of the book, I came to the determination not to include them. My thoughts along this line were that throughout Lar's career as an author, he was always very careful not to present too much in the way of speculation, but rather, Lar concentrated on presenting factual information from documented sources and photographic examples of the various artifact types being discussed. I felt that to include certain gorget styles and birdstones would necessitate a higher degree of speculation on the part of the author in linking their use directly to the atl-atl than was acceptable, so the decision was made to limit the artifacts included to only those that have a known association — whether utilitarian or ceremonial in nature — with the atl-atl.

Although I personally have many questions and thoughts with regard to bannerstones being or not being clan totems or status symbols, whether certain gorgets were used as weights, and whether or not birdstones were actually used as a component part to some types of atl-atls as seen on some pre-Columbian carved examples, the purpose of this book is not to put forward my own personal speculations and extrapolations (which are greatly limited when compared to the life-long study of more noted authors). Rather, as stated in the beginning paragraph, the object of this book is to present photographic examples of bannerstones and related artifacts from many private collections around the country for other collectors to view and enjoy.

Atl-atls, Weights & Bannerstones

Over 14,000 years ago as Paleo man traveled the continent now known as North America, he hunted with long thrusting spears tipped with flaked points. Hunting with such weapons was often dangerous as the hunters would need to approach very close to their prey in order to strike it with enough impact for their spears to pierce the animal's tough hide and with enough force to penetrate deep enough to strike a vital organ.

During the middle to late Paleo period, ancient man developed a new weapon called the atl-atl. Held in one hand, this spear thrower would launch a spear approximately six feet in length at its intended target. The use of this tool allowed the spear to travel faster and farther than hand thrown spears, while it allowed the hunters to remain at a safer distance from their prey when launching their spears. At the end of this spear was a smaller point, usually made of flint, called a dart point.

The atl-atl is simple in design, being a smoothed stick around 16" to 24" in length with a handle at one end and a hook made from antler at the other end. One end of the spear was placed against the hook, and when released or flung, the thrower would launch the spear at distances and speeds far exceeding that which could be achieved without the use of the thrower. During the Archaic period, perforated bannerstones begin to appear in the archaeological record, yet for some unknown reason, their use did not continue into later time periods.

3¼" drilled bannerstone found in Warren Co., NC. Collection of Cliff Jackson. $400.00 – 500.00

While the atl-atl is an effective working weapon system with just the main shaft, hook, and spear, many atl-atls made in ancient times utilized a counter-balance weight attached at the center of the shaft. I have used examples with weights and without, and I find the weighted system does in fact work better than the unweighted. Weights came in various shapes and sizes and were made from various locally found materials. The method of attachment to the main shaft is the predominate difference between the various types of weights. While there are various styles that were tied directly to the main shaft, there were also those utilizing a drilled hole (perforation) in the center of the weight called bannerstones which are main subject of this book.

Even with all of the study that has been completed over the last 100 years, the whole story behind some artifact types remains illusive, and bannerstones are one such type of artifact. Some artifacts, when professionally excavated, are found in such a way that their story is literally laid out around them, plain to see. A gorget or pendant found sitting on the chest of a skeletal remain is pretty good evidence that it was worn as an ornament around the neck. Conch shell ornaments found on either side of a skull is a good indication they were worn as ear decoration. A flint point found hafted into a fore-shaft is solid evidence it was used in conjunction with an atl-atl. Excavating and documenting such in situ finds is what has provided the collector with much of the knowledge we have about many of the artifacts we collect. There are certain types of artifacts however, that even though found in situ, only paint a partial picture of their whole story in ancient times. With the bannerstone group, it has been well documented that they have been found in association with other atl-atl components, namely the atl-atl hook that was attached to the end of the spear thrower and the atl-atl handle that was attached to the opposite end. When looking at the size of the drilled hole that perforates the middle of a bannerstone, it is not hard to draw the conclusion that the bannerstone was hafted to the center of the atl-atl shaft between the hook and handle.

Atl-atl hooks and handles are rare items to find as the moisture in most areas will have caused the antler material they were made from to have rotted away long ago. Atl-atl hooks pictured here are from the collection of Charlie Wagers. Museum Grade.

Gary Fogelman, editor of Indian Artifact Magazine and world champion atl-atl competition thrower demonstrating the use of an atl-atl.

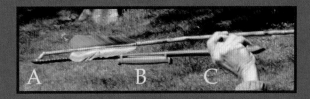

Close-up view of an atl-atl made to replicate those used in ancient times.

6⅝" atl-atl hook made in ancient times from deer antler. Photo courtesy of the Museum of Native American Artifacts, Bentonville, AR. $1,400.00 – 2,000.00

Group of four ancient atl-atl spear dart points still hafted to their original foreshafts. These foreshafts would have inserted into the end of the atl-atl spear. Photo courtesy of the Museum of Native American Artifacts, Bentonville, AR. $2,000.00 – 3,000.00 each

Atl-atl handle made from antler with a drilled hole where the main shaft of the atl-atl would have been inserted. Photo courtesy of the Museum of Native American Artifacts, Bentonville, AR. $250.00 – 400.00

Antler hook and bannerstone set found together in Henderson Co, Kentucky. Bannerstone is made from limestone. Collection of Charlie Wagers. Museum Grade

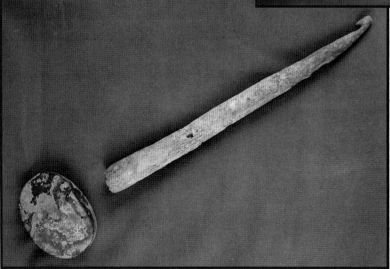

Found in Spencer Co., Indiana, in a the crib mound. Antler hook is 7¾" long and bannerstone is 2¼" (Green River style). Collection of Charlie Wagers. Museum Grade

6⅛" antler hook and 4" drilled antler bannerstone (very rare) found at the Chiggerville site in Ohio Co., KY. Collection of Charlie Wagers. Museum Grade

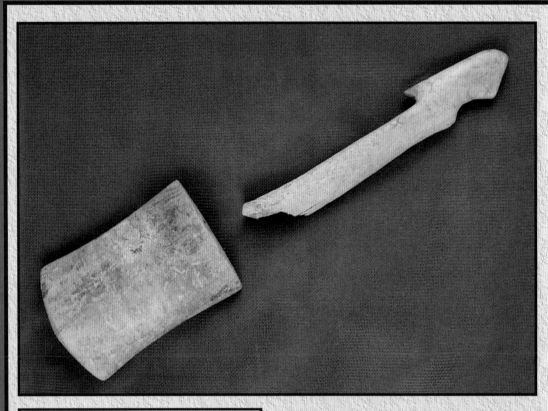

4⅞" antler hook and 3" saddle bannerstone found in overflow pond site Warrick Co., IN. Collection of Charlie Wagers. Museum Grade

Bannerstones, as well as other types of tied-on weights were made in a wide range of shapes and styles. While various different materials that were locally available were used in their manufacture, slate was by far the most common. Green banded glacial slate, red slate, and black slate were all used in crafting bannerstones in ancient times. Used less often in ancient times but still found are banners made from various hardstone and other types of material such as chlorite, granite, diorite, and hematite, as well as quartzite. In the more southern regions like Mississippi and Alabama up to Kentucky and even farther north, bannerstones are often found made from siltstone or claystone.

The bannerstones in this chapter are not listed in chronological order according to time period, but rather in random order to show the vast variations in styles. We have used the names associated with the various types most often used by collectors.

Examples of Drilled Bannerstones

Ball Banners	Pick Banners
Winged Banners	Giniculates
Tube Banners	Panel Banners
"D" Banners	Shuttle Banners
Saddleback Banners	Benton Style Banners
Hourglass Banners	Prismoidal
Bottle Banners	Reel Banners

Winged Banners

One of the more common styles of bannerstones are the winged varieties. Winged banners vary in width from one to the next, with some having shorter wings and others, such as the "wing nut" style having long, tapering wings.

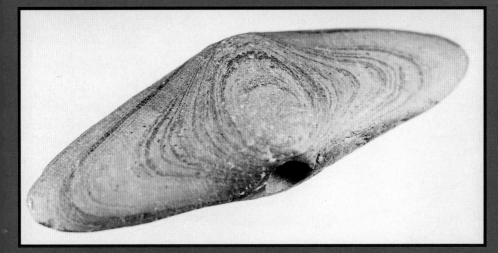

4¾" winged bannerstone found in Richland Co., OH. Made from brownish banded slate. Doug Hooks collection. $475.00

5¾" winged bannerstone found in Richland Co., OH. Doug Hooks collection. $800.00

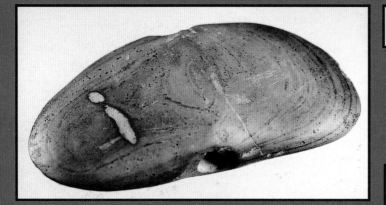

4½" winged bannerstone found in Ashland, Co., OH, in 1984 by Bob Bright. Personal Find

4¹/₁₆" long winged bannerstone found in Fairfield Co., OH. G. Thrush collection. $450.00

4¼" winged bannerstone made from quartzite. Unique tally marks on banner wings. Found in Columbiana Co., OH. Collection of Alan Selders. Price not listed.

7¼" winged bannerstone made from green slate. Found in Wood Co., OH. Collection of Sam Speck. $2,500.00

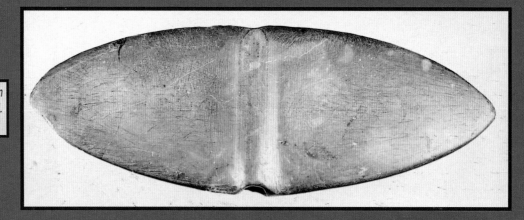

4⅝" winged bannerstone found in Champaign Co., OH. Ex. Vietzen. Collection of Alan Selders. $1,200.00

4⅛" winged bannerstone made from hardstone. Found in Hardin Co., OH. Collection of Alan Selders. Museum Grade

4⅜" winged bannerstone found in Knox Co., OH. Collection of Alan Selders. $1,500.00

4¾" winged bannerstone found in Holmes Co., OH. Ex. Weiss, ex. Wengard. Collection of Alan Selders. $650.00

5¾" winged bannerstone preform found in Auglaize Co., OH. Wings and barrel have been shaped, but drilling had not started. Gene Edwards collection. $300.00

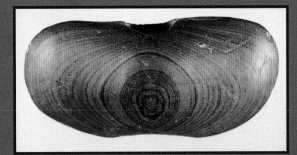

2¹⁵⁄₁₆" winged bannerstone found in Logan Co., OH. Ex. M. Van Steen. Collection of Fred Winegardner. $750.00

4⅜" winged bannerstone found in Knox Co., OH. Ex. Jim Hawks, ex. Jack Roberts. Collection of Charlie Fulk. $800.00

4⅞" winged bannerstone found in Williams Co., OH. Ex. Snyder. Collection of Charlie Fulk. $1,100.00

4⅞" winged bannerstone found in Montcalm Co., MI. Ex. Phillips, ex. Tolliver. Collection of Charlie Fulk. $1,200.00

4⅜" winged bannerstone found in Ross Co., OH. Ex. Jim Hawks, ex. Jack Roberts. Collection of Charlie Fulk. $1,200.00

3⅝" winged bannerstone found in Eaton Co., MI. Collection of Dave Yallup. $1,500.00

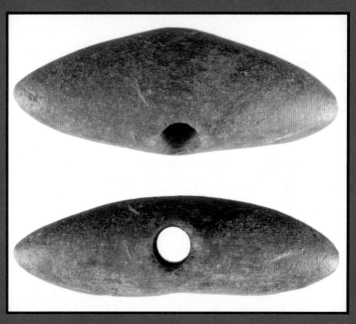

3¾" greenstone wing banner found by Cliff Jackson in Warren Co., NC. Personal Find

3¼" winged bannerstone found in Highland Co., OH. Collection of Mike Barron. $700.00

3½" wide x 1½" long bannerstone made from siltstone. Found in South Alabama. $750.00

2¼" x 1¼" winged bannersotne found in Fulton Co., OH. Collection of Dennis Link. $700.00

3¼" x 2¾" winged bannerstone found in Licking Co., OH. Ex Meuser. Collection of Dennis Link. $1,500.00

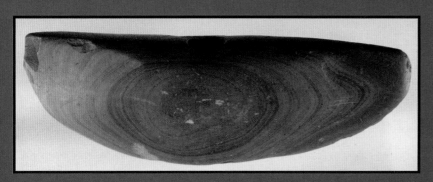

4½" x 1½" winged bannerstone found in Mahoning Co., OH. Eric Wagner collection. $800.00

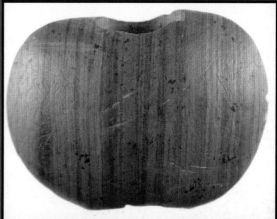

2¼" long x 1¾" wide winged bannerstone found in Coshocton Co., OH. Collection of Jon Dickinson. $500.00

4" winged bannerstone made from hardstone. Found in McCracken Co., KY. Gary Noel collection. $5,000.00

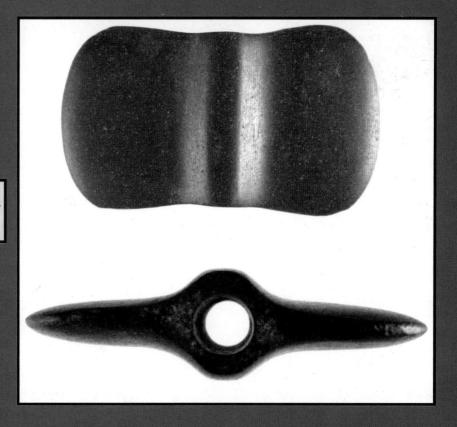

4⅜" winged bannerstone made from hardstone and found in McCracken Co., KY. Gary Noel collection. $3,500.00

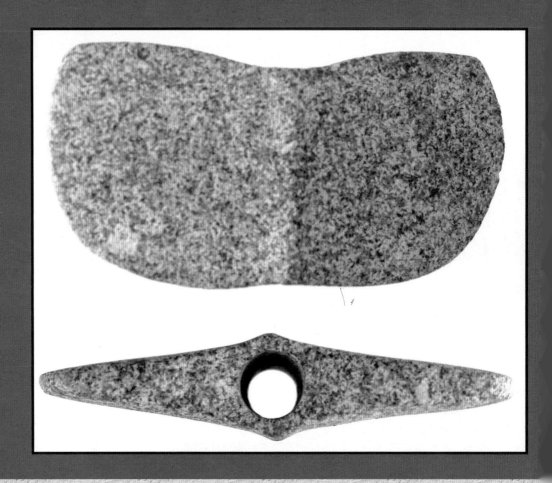

Double Bit Axe Banners

Similar to the winged bannerstones in shape is a style called the double bit axe banner. These bannerstones are longer than wide, and both wings taper in thickness.

5" double bitted axe bannerstone made from banded slate. Found in Franklin Co., OH. Collection of Doug Hooks. $350.00

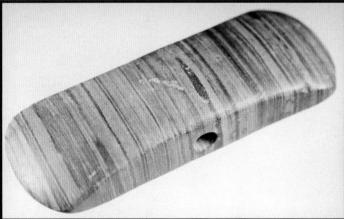

5½" double bitted axe bannerstone found in central Ohio. Made from nicely banded glacial slate. Doug Hooks collection. Museum Grade

4⅛" double bitted axe bannerstone found in Washington Co., OH. Ex. Wehrle #2365. Collection of Alan Selders. $1,500.00

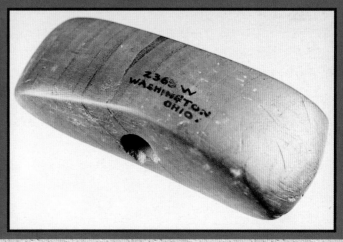

Ball Banners

Ball bannerstones are completely round, or almost round in shape and most have a "fluted" or grooved side. When placed on the atl-atl shaft, this fluted side would have faced up, I believe, in order to allow the main shaft of the atl-atl spear to rest in, or just above, the groove so that the body of this otherwise round weight would not interfere with the launching of the spear.

1⅞" fluted ball bannerstone found in Knox Co., OH. Collection of Fred Winegardner. $450.00

1½" diameter fluted ball bannerstone made from slate, found in Belle Point, OH. Doug Hooks collection. $500.00

2" diameter fluted ball bannerstone found in Ashland Co., OH. Ex. Jim Hawks. Collection of Doug Hooks. $800.00

1⅝" long fluted ball bannerstone found in Ohio. This example has an elongated shape but still falls in the ball banner classification. Ex. Jack Hooks collection. Collection of Doug Hooks. $350.00

2⅝" fluted ball bannerstone found in Knox Co., OH. Sam Speck collection. Museum Grade

1⅝" wide fluted ball bannerstone found in Ohio. Collection Alan Selders. $450.00

1⅞" fluted ball bannerstone found in Fairfield Co., OH. Don Casto collection. $550.00

1⅞" diameter nicely polished fluted ball bannerstone found in Franklin Co., OH. Ex. Stanley Copeland and Dick Coulter collections. Currently in the collection of Doug Hooks. $750.00

2" ball bannerstone found in Ohio. Collection of Lar Hothem. $350.00

Ball bannerstone found in Midwest. Collection of David & Aaron Kilander. Museum Grade

2" x 1½" fluted ball banner-stone found in Ohio. Collection of Dennis Link. $1,000.00

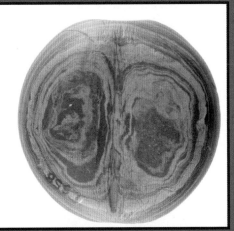

2" x 2" fluted ball bannerstone found in Ohio. Collection of Dennis Link. $1,500.00

2¼" x 1½" fluted ball bannerstone found in Preble Co., OH. Collection of Dennis Link. $1,000.00

1¾" x 1½" fluted ball bannerstone found in Jay Co., IN. Collection of Dennis Link. $750.00

2" long x 1⅜" tall fluted ball bannerstone found in Ohio. Collection Jon Dickinson. $1,500.00

1¾" x 1¼" fluted ball bannerstone found in Ohio. Collection of Dennis Link. $900.00

Tube Banners

Tube banners are named due to their tubular style, and can be round, have a flattened bottom, or a fluted bottom similar to the flutes found in ball bannerstones. As with ball banners, I believe the flat or fluted side would have faced up when attached to the atl-atl shaft so as to not interfere with the spear shaft when launching. Tube banners are round and cylindrical, with some examples tapering from one end to the other.

2¼" drilled bannerstone made from chlorite, found in the Midwest. This is a rare material type. Collection of Doug Hooks. $750.00

4⅞" tube bannerstone that is fully drilled, however the holes did not meet in the center properly. The crafter left the exterior surface with visible pecking marks since the final polish was not done due to the mismatched hole drilling. Found in Richland Co., OH. Doug Hooks collection. $150.00

3⅝" tube bannerstone made from brown slate, fluted on two sides and nicely polished, found in Crawford Co., OH, in 1945. Doug Hooks collection. $1,200.00

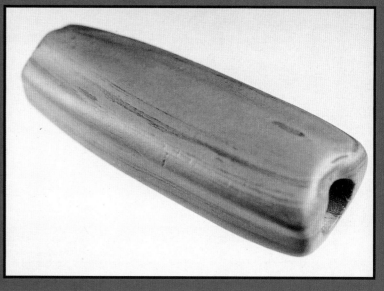

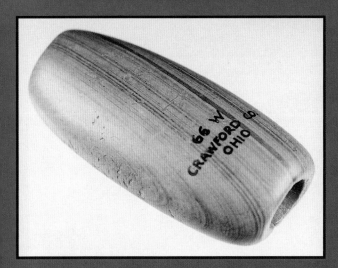

3¼" tube bannerstone found in Crawford Co., OH. Ex. Wehrle, ex. McKnight, ex. Babst. Collection of Doug Hooks. $1,200.00

4¹⁄₁₆" tube bannerstone found in Vermillion Co., IN. Ex. Cain. Collection of Doug Hooks. $800.00

3½" fluted tube bannerstone found in Delaware Co., OH. Ex. Root. Collection of Doug Hooks. $750.00

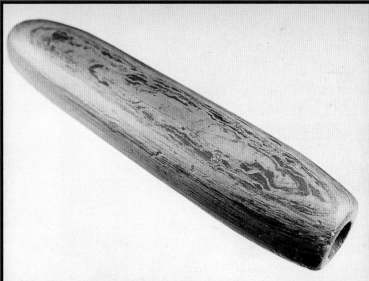

6½" fluted tube bannerstone found in Ashland Co., OH. Ex. Jim Hawks. Found in 1929. Collection of Sam Speck. Museum Grade

2⅞" tube bannerstone found in Ohio. Collection of Alan Selders. $500.00

4⅛" long tube bannerstone found in Montgomery Co., OH. Ex. Meuser #1469/5. Collection of Alan Selders. Museum Grade

3⅛" fluted tube bannerstone found Holmes Co., OH. Collection of Alan Selders. $450.00

4½" fluted tube bannerstone found in Holmes Co., OH. Ex. Wengard. Collection of Alan Selders. $550.00

2⅞" tube bannerstone found in Holmes Co., OH. Ex. Wengard. Collection of Alan Selders. $250.00

4" fluted tube bannerstone found in Ohio. Collection of Charlie Fulk. $500.00

2⅝" fluted tube bannerstone found near Mt. Gilead, OH. Collection of Charlie Fulk. $500.00

5¾" tube bannerstone found in Ashland Co., OH. Collection of Charlie Fulk. $750.00

4" tube bannerstone found in Indiana. Gene Edwards collection. $500.00

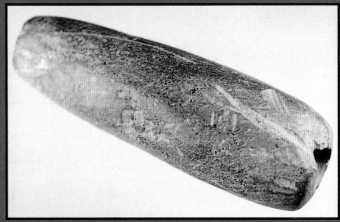

4⅛" tube bannerstone, partially drilled. Found in Seneca Co., OH. Gene Edwards collection. $350.00

5" tube bannerstone found in Adams Co., IN. Surface exhibits original pecking with no polish. Gene Edwards collection. $350.00

5⁹⁄₁₆" tube bannerstone, partially drilled. Found in Ohio. Gene Edwards collection. $250.00

4½" tapered tube bannerstone found in Scioto Co., OH. Gene Edwards collection. $350.00

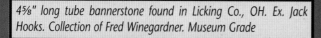

4⅝" long tube bannerstone found in Licking Co., OH. Ex. Jack Hooks. Collection of Fred Winegardner. Museum Grade

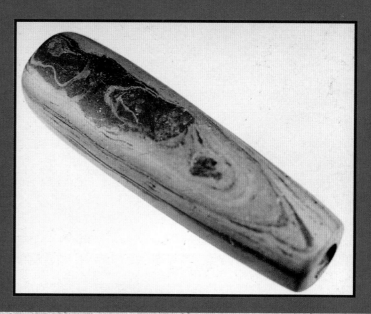

2¾" tube bannerstone found in Ashland Co., OH. Collection of Charlie Fulk. $550.00

2¾" tube bannerstone found in Erie Co., OH. Ex. Meuser #3563/5, ex. Speck. Collection of Fred Winegardner. $450.00

2" long x 1¼" wide fluted tube banner-stone made from inudated siltstone. Found in southwest Georgia. $700.00

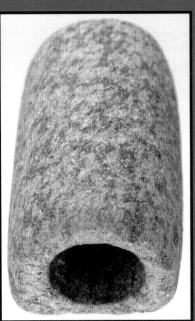

4¾" tube bannerstone found in Indiana. Collection of Gene Edwards. $450.00

Very rare style 3" x 1½" stylized tube bannerstone found in OH. Collection of Dennis Link. $1,500.00

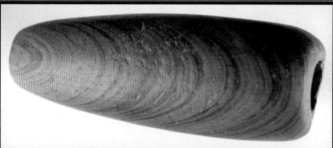

3½" x 1½" tube bannerstone that tapers in width from one end to the other. Found in Ohio. Collection of Dennis Link. $600.00

3" fluted tube bannerstone found in southeastern Illinois. Ex. Norbert Bingman. Lar Hothem collection. $900.00

3⅜" tube bannerstone found in southeastern Illinois with a flattened top. Ex. Norbert Bingman. Lar Hothem collection. $500.00

Pick Banners

Pick bannerstones are longer than wide and come in varying lengths with both ends tapering to a point. Most all picks are fairly thick around the middle where the hole was drilled.

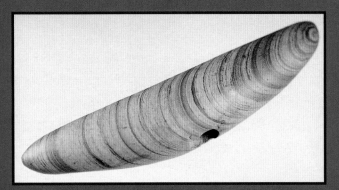

Pick bannerstone found in Licking Co., OH. Ex. Shipley, ex. Steve Hart. Doug Hooks collection. $3,500.00

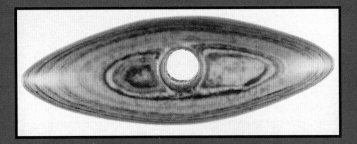

3⁵⁄₁₆" pick bannerstone found in Franklin Co., OH. Ex. Dunn. Collection of Doug Hooks. $750.00

4⅞" pick bannerstone found in Lorain Co., OH. Made from heavily patinated banded slate. Collection of Doug Hooks. $1,000.00

4½" pick bannerstone found in Marion Co., OH. Ex. Driskill, pictured in Who's Who #2. Collection of Doug Hooks. $1,200.00

2½" pick bannerstone found in Coshocton Co., OH. Collection of Alan Selders. $750.00

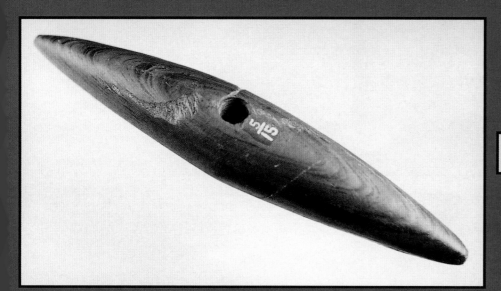

6½" pick bannerstone found in Logan Co., OH. Collection of Charlie Fulk. $1,700.00

3¹⁄₁₆" pick bannerstone found in Delaware Co., OH. Collection of Fred Winegardner. $650.00

3" pick bannerstone found in Ohio. Collection of Fred Winegardner. $700.00

6" x 1" pick bannerstone found in Senaca Co., OH. Ex Meuser. Collection of Dennis Link. $2,500.00

3¾" x 1¼" pick bannerstone found in Henry Co., IN. Collection of Dennis Link. $650.00

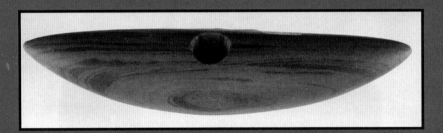

4¾" x 1¼" pick bannerstone found in Blackford Co., IN. Collection of Dennis Link. $1,200.00

3½" x 1¼" Franklin Co., OH. Ex Meusor. $800.00

5⅞" pick bannerstone made from hardstone (rare for type) Found in western Kentucky. Collection of Gary Noel. Museum Grade

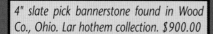

4" slate pick bannerstone found in Wood Co., Ohio. Lar hothem collection. $900.00

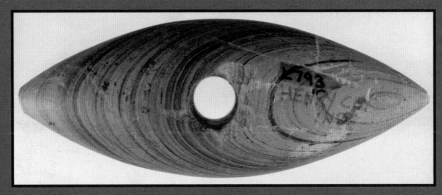

3¾" x 1¼" pick bannerstone found in Ohio. Collection of Dennis Link. $600.00

6¾" x 1¾" pick bannerstone found in Ohio. Ex Wachtel. Collection of Dennis Link. Museum Grade

Geniculates

One of the stranger styles in the bannerstone family are geniculates. With their very distinct "L" shape and elongated or oblong perforation hole, these bannerstones are easy to identify due to their unique design.

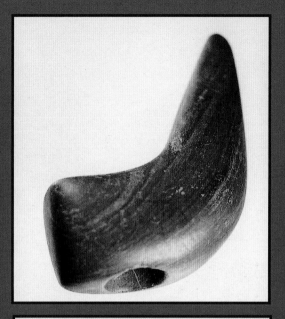

3¼" geniculate found in Ohio. Collection of Charlie Fulk. Museum Grade

3⅛" geniculate bannerstone found in Marion Co., OH. Doug Hooks collection. $2,250.00

2¼" long truncated geniculate found in Ohio. Ex. Payne, ex. B. W. Stephens, ex. Parks. Pictured in the Bannerstone Book, page 349. Collection of Bob Bright. Museum Grade

4³⁄₁₆" geniculate found in Noble Co., OH. Made from nicely banded glacial slate. Collection of Doug Hooks. $3,500.00

3⅝" x 2⅝" geniculate found in Kentucky. Collection of Alan Selders. Museum Grade

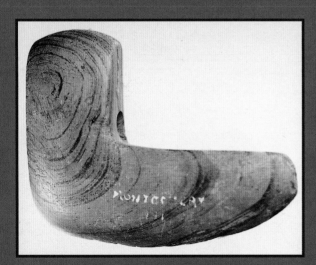

3⅛" geniculate found in Montgomery Co., OH. This piece has been broken and glued at the hole, reducing its optimum value. Gene Edwards collection. $200.00

2" x 1½" geniculate found in Ohio. Ex Meuser. Collection of Dennis Link. $1,200.00

2¼" x 2" geniculate found in Williams Co., OH. Ex Meuser. Collection of Dennis Link. $800.00

4" long x 2½" tall geniculate found in Ohio. Ex. Dr. Hicks, ex. Shipley Lot 31018. Collection of Jon Dickinson. $900.00

3⅝" geniculate found in Indiana. Collection of David and Aaron Kilander. Museum Grade

Panel Banners

While virtually all bannerstones had a round perforation hole, panel banners had an elongated hole of the same design as the geniculates, making the panel banner variety easy to identify. Panel banners have short wings that taper in thickness towards their ends.

2⅛" panel bannerstone found in Seneca Co., OH. Ex. Tolliver, ex. Baumgardner. Collection of Charlie Fulk. $900.00

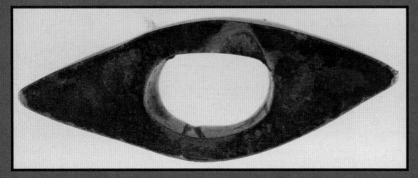

2⅛" x ⅝" tall panel, Licking Co., OH. Gift to Charles Fritz 6/5/69. Collection of Jon Dickinson. $650.00

1¾" x 1" panel bannerstone found in Logan Co., OH. Collection of Dennis Link. $600.00

2¼" x 2" panel bannerstone found in Ohio. Collection of Dennis Link. $1,350.00

2¼" x 1" panel bannerstone found in Ohio. Collection of Dennis Link. $600.00

Other Style Banners

1¾" claystone bannerstone found in the Midwest. This piece has unique tally marks on the lower edges. Doug Hooks collection. $350.00

2⅞" wide shuttle bannerstone found in Ohio. Ex. Dunn, ex. Kiel, ex. Jack Hooks. Pictured in Who's Who #7 and #9. Doug Hooks collection. $700.00

2⅜" wide drilled bannerstone found in Muskingum Co., OH. Courtesy of Back to Earth Rocks & Relics. $350.00

3½" semi-finished bannerstone made from granite, found in Barren Co., KY. Ex. Gary Noel. Collection of Bob Bright. $450.00

3½" bannerstone found in Ashland Co., OH. Collection of Bob Bright. $800.00

2¾" long hardstone bannerstone pictured in Who's Who #1. Collection of Doug Hooks. $1,500.00

3¾" bannerstone found in Harrison Co., OH. Ex. Black. Collection of Alan Selders. Museum Grade

2" long bannerstone found in Hocking Co., OH. This is an exceptionally rare bannerstone style. Collection of Alan Selders. Museum Grade

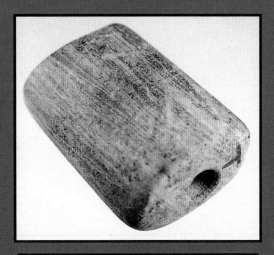

2¹⁄₁₆" bannerstone found in Ohio. Gene Edwards collection. $450.00

4¼" bannerstone found in Butler Co., OH. Gene Edwards collection. $850.00

2¾" bannerstone found in Muskingum Co., OH. Larry Garvin collection. $400.00

3" wide bannerstone found in Ohio. Don Casto collection. $550.00

2¾" winged bannerstone that is drilled with a partially finished surface. Found in Shelby Co., IN. Larry Garvin collection. $225.00

2¾" bannerstone that is drilled with a partially finished surface. Found in Shelby Co., IN. Back to Earth Rocks & Relics. $225.00

2½" bannerstone with an unusually small center hole that only measures ⅜" diameter. Found in Richland Co., OH. Collection of Charlie Fulk. $600.00

3⅜" winged bannerstone found in Ashland Co., OH. Ex. Swartz. Collection of Charlie Fulk. $1,000.00

3⅝" bannerstone found in Ashland Co., OH. Ex. Steve Fuller. Collection of Charlie Fulk. $1,200.00

3⅝" x 1⅞" bannerstone found in Eaton Co., MI. Collection of Dave Yallup. Museum Grade

2½" x 2⅜" bannerstone preform that has been shaped and polished, but the drilling was never completed. Found in Illinois. Collection of Lar Hothem. $250.00

2⅜" x 2¾" partially drilled bannerstone preform. Found in Meade Co., KY. Collection of Lar Hothem. $300.00

3⅛" long bannerstone preform found in Ohio. Collection of Gene Edwards. $250.00

3⅛" bannerstone that is not only drilled, but also has a tie-on groove. Found in Sandusky Co., OH. Ex. Vietzen. Collection of Gene Edwards. $350.00

2¼" bannerstone found in Marshall Co., KY. Collection of Gary Noel. Museum Grade

3¼" wide bannerstone found in Warren Co., NC. Cliff Jackson collection. $450.00

2" long x 1¼" wide Benton Culture bannerstone made from steatite. Found in Tallapoosa Co., AL. Charles Ray collection. $750.00

3" x 2½" bannerstone made from banded slate. Found in northeast Mississippi. Charles Ray collection. $3,500.00

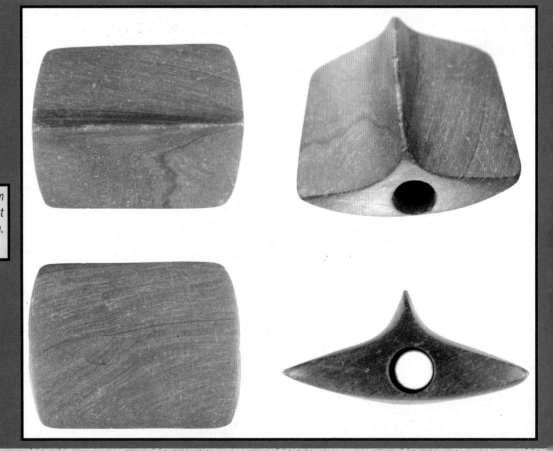

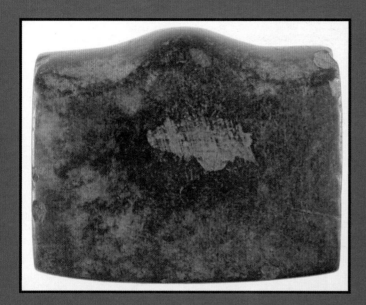

1¾" long x 1¼" wide Benton Culture bannerstone made from limonite. Found in Dallas Co., AL. Charles Ray collection. $2,000.00

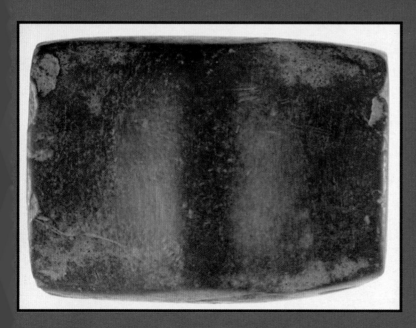

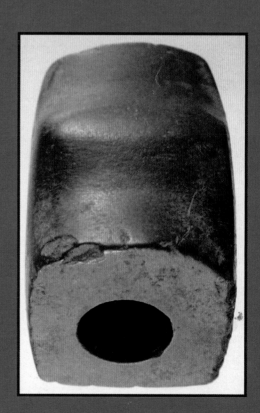

2" long x 2" wide bannerstone, siltstone, south Alabama. Benton Culture. Charles Ray collection. $1,200.00

Bannerstone, 1¾" x 1¾", limonite. Charles Ray collection. $1,200.00

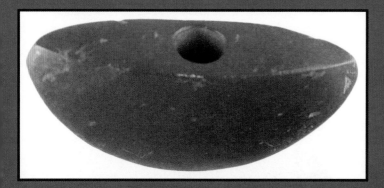

3½" wide x 1½" long siltstone bannerstone, south Alabama. Charles Ray collection. $750.00

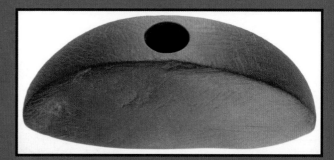

3¼" wide x 1½" long siltstone bannerstone, south Alabama. Charles Ray collection. $750.00

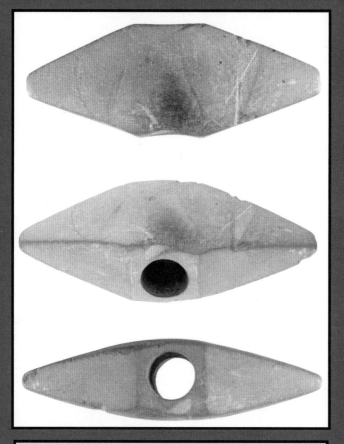

3½" wide x 1¼" long bannerstone, greenstone, northeast Mississippi. Charles Ray collection. $500.00

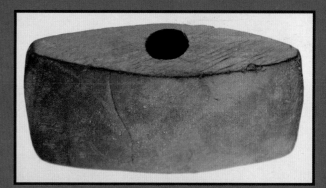

3¼" x 1¾" siltstone bannerstone, south Alabama. Charles Ray collection. $350.00

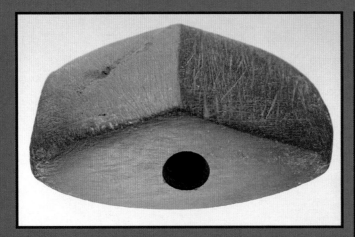

Bannerstone, 2½" x 2", south Georgia. Charles Ray collection. $500.00

1¾" x 1⅛" siltstone bannerstone, south Georgia. Charles Ray collection. $125.00

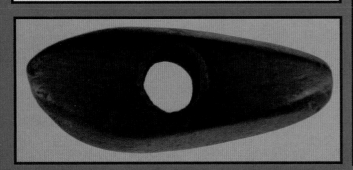

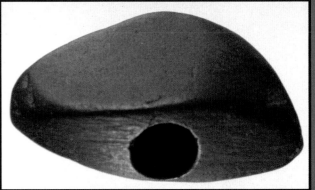

2¼" x 1⅜" clay baked bannerstone, south Alabama. Charles Ray collection. $125.00

Engraved banner (salvaged), 2¼" long x ¾" thick. Bladen Co., NC. Dennis Hess collection. $200.00

1½" x 1½" Clermont Co., OH. Ex. Shipley, ex. Hillen. Dennis Hess collection. $500.00

5" x 1¾" Franklin Co., OH. Ex. Kientz, ex. Shipley. Dennis Hess collection. $800.00

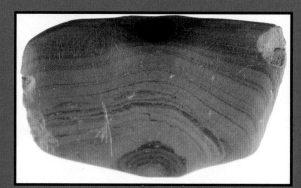

Banner, Lake Co., OH, 3" x 2¼". Eric Wagner collection. $500.00

Banner, found in Ohio, 3" x 1¾". Eric Wagner collection. $900.00

Banner, Medina Co., OH, 2¾" x 2¼". Eric Wagner collection. $175.00

Bannerstone (Green River oval), hardstone, 3" wide. Gary Noel collection. $4,500.00

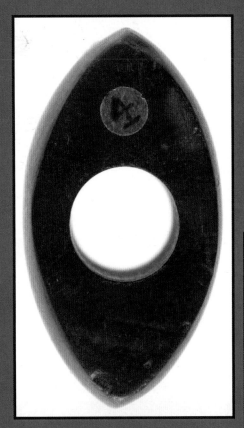

Benton humped bannerstone, claystone, Hardin Co., TN, 2¼". Gary Noel collection. $600.00

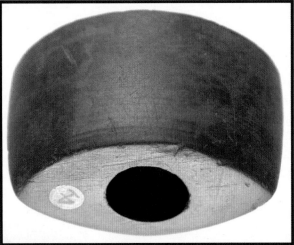

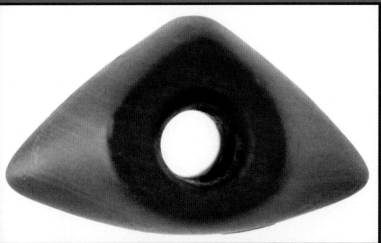

Bottle bannerstone, claystone, Critenden Co., KY, 2⅝". Gary Noel collection. $3,000.00

2¼" hourglass bannerstone found in southern Illinois. Ex. Bingman collection Lar Hothem collection. $1,200.00

3½" winged bannerstone found in Illinois. Ex. Bingman. Lar Hothem collection. $450.00

3½" hardstone "D" bannerstone, found in Barren Co., Kentucky. Lar Hothem collection. $800.00

Saddle barb preform, 2⅛" long x 2" wide, Indiana. D. Warner. Jon Dickinson collection. $200.00

2⅜" x 1⅞" bannerstone, Indiana. Museum of Native American Artifacts. $1,250.00

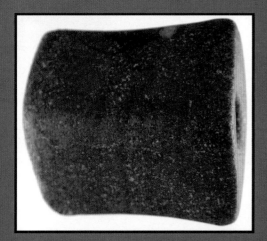

2¼" x 2" bannerstone, Indiana. $2,500.00

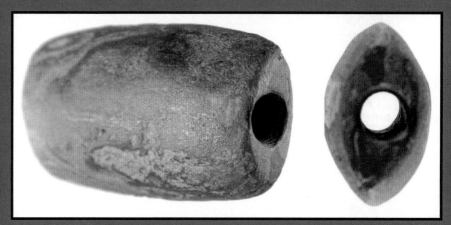

2¾" bannerstone found in Kentucky. Monty Pennington collection. $700.00

Beautiful quartz bannerstone. Monty Pennington collection. Museum Grade

Small unnotched wing, 2½" long x 1⅛" wide, New London, OH. Jon Dickinson collection. $500.00

Clarksville banner, 2¾", granite material, Breckenridge Co., KY. Archaic collected from finder. Monty Pennington collection. Museum Grade.

Dell type, 3½" long x 1⅜" tall, found 4 miles southwest of Bowling Green, OH. #87515 Mueser. Jon Dickinson collection. $5,000.00

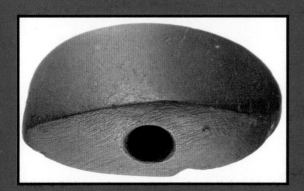

Bannerstone, 2⅛" x 1⅛", siltstone. Charles Ray collection. $200.00

Reel banner, 1½" x 2¼", archaic, Garrard Co., KY. Ex. Clem Caldwell. Jon Dickinson collection. Museum Grade.

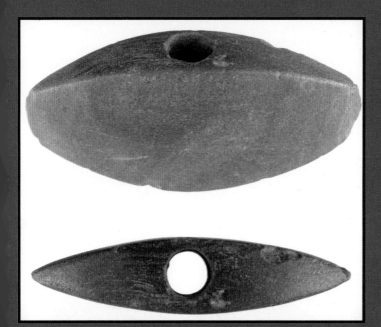

Bannerstone, 4½" wide x 1¼" long, north Mississippi. Charles Ray collection. $700.00

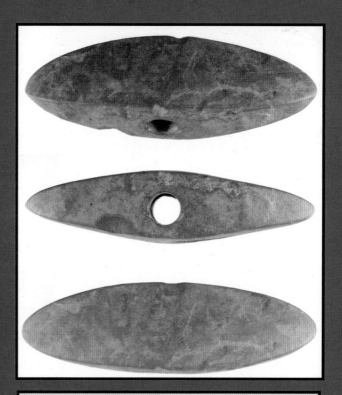

Bannerstone, 3¾" wide x 1⅝" long, south Georgia. Charles Ray collection. $800.00

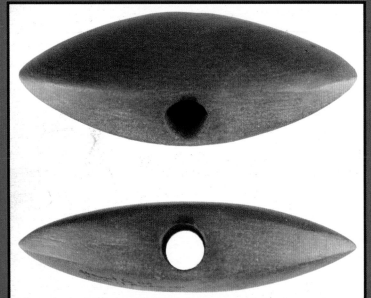

Bannerstone, 4½" wide x 1⅝" long, south Alabama. Charles Ray collection. $1,200.00

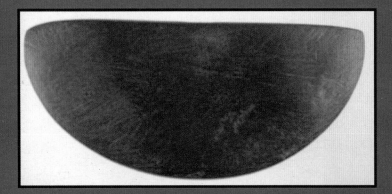

3¼" bannerstone made from siltstone. Found in southern Alabama. Collection of Charles Ray. $750.00

Bannerstone, 3⅛" wide x 1¼" long, siltstone, Mississippi. Charles Ray collection. $800.00

Bannerstone, 2½" wide x 1" long, siltstone, south Alabama. Charles Ray collection. $400.00

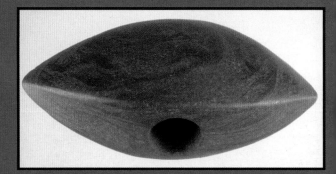

Bannerstone, 2¾" wide x 1⅝" long, south Alabama. Charles Ray collection. $450.00

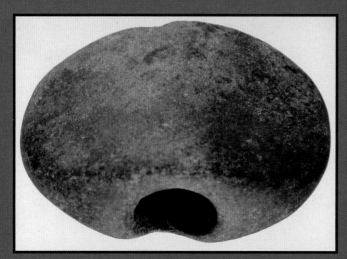

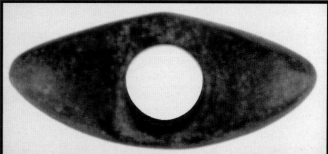

Bannerstone, 1⅞" x 1¼", hardstone. Charles Ray collection. $175.00

Bannerstone, 3" x 1½", siltstone, south Alabama, restored corner. Charles Ray collection. $300.00

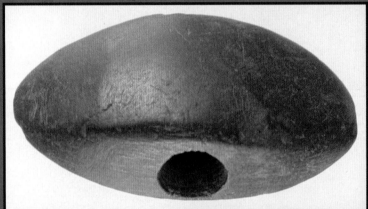

Bannerstone, 2" x 1¼", siltstone, south Alabama. Charles Ray collection. $125.00

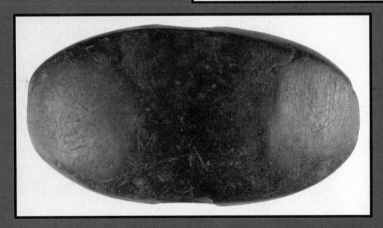

Reel type bannerstone found in Bowling Green, Wood Co., OH. Ex. Meuser #875/5. Jon Dickinson collection. Museum Grade

Utilitarian or Ceremonial?

Butterflies, Ovates, Lunates & Crescents

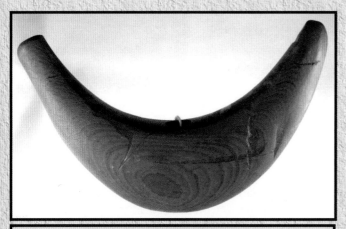

5⅜" x 3½" lunate found in Hardin Co., OH. Ex. Parks. Collection of Dennis Link. $3,500.00

For decades it has been surmised that the banner-stone is a counter-balance weight that was placed at the center of the atl-atl shaft to improve the optimum ability of the weapon. Another line of thought is that more elaborate bannerstones were places on the ends of staffs to designate status or tribal affiliation. The documentation that has previous been published about bannerstones leads one to conclude the bannerstone was in fact associated with the atl-atl spear thrower. Yet, when looking at some of the more ornate bannerstones, questions arise as to the possibility that such pieces could stand the torque generated by the thrower during daily use. Another valid question has always been, why put so much time and energy into making such an elaborate component part, when its use was purely utilitarian? Thus, the question remains — was the bannerstone a component part of a functional atl-atl weapon, or was it manufactured with an intended use of being a part of a ceremony or burial ritual? Several examples of the more ornately designed double crescents and notched ovates were drilled in such a way that a shaft placed through the perforation would not be able to be inserted completely though both sides of the outer notches, leading one to believe these were either never attached to a shaft or the bannerstone was simply placed on the end of the shaft which acted as a staff.

More than one previous author has addressed the fact that many of the styles of bannerstones that are found simply would not hold up to the stress of daily use.

This leads one to surmise such items were designed and manufactured purely for ceremonial use. Without the benefit of a written history, we can only speculate at the exact nature of the ancient ceremonies that took place, as well as the nature of the spiritual beliefs of the people who lived in ancient times. We do know from archaeological excavations that during the archaic time period when bannerstones were being manufactured, ancient man did place "grave goods" in the burials of the deceased. And it has also been well documented (especially by Lutz) that bannerstones have been excavated in association with burials leaving a person hard pressed to deny that bannerstones did in fact have a ceremonial significance. But did all bannerstones have such a significance? There in lies the question at the heart of the bannerstone debate — were all styles purely ceremonial? Were all styles utilitarian? Were some component atl-atl parts, while others were ceremonial in nature?

When studying mortuary practices of ancient cultures around the world, one of the most common traits associated with the burial of the departed is the placement of various objects in the grave. Some of the more documented ancient cultures in various corners of the world left a written record which more clearly explains that such goods were there to assist the deceased with their journey into the next world. The sacrificing of servants being the most extreme example of the belief that things from this world could be taken into the next. Yet, simply because one culture in one time period in one part of the world held such a belief, certainly does not mean that all goods placed in graves in all time periods in all parts of the world were part of that belief. The fact is, that as of the writing of this book, the placement of grave goods with the deceased continues as an everyday occurrence in the United States. From golf tees to favorite books to even Indian artifacts, objects are quite frequently placed along with the deceased before interment. None of which are done for use in the "next life," but rather as a part of a ritualistic goodbye done more to assist the mourners cope with the death of a loved one than for any other reason. The point is, not every thing that is found, excavated, uncovered, or studied has to have a deeper significance. Often, we as travelers in the twenty-first century have to content ourselves with the fact that there are simply certain aspects of the past that will never be known to us. The intricacies of ancient ceremonies and spiritual beliefs being one of those aspects. True, it is fun to hypothesize and theorize, and often with much study and observation of the artifacts and their insitu associations very valid arguments can be made — but the bottom line is, there is no way to turn such arguments into factual conclusions in many circumstances. In the year 2450 AD the golf tees that were found in a casket buried in 2010 were not placed there to assist the deceased with his game in the next world. They were there because the deceased liked to golf. The box of Winchester anniversary edition 12 gauge shotgun shells were not placed there to assist with future hunts in the next life, they were placed there because when he couldn't golf in the winter, the deceased loved to go duck hunting.

While my personal beliefs are that it is very possible, and even probable, that some items were in fact placed in graves as offerings to unknown deities, and other objects very well may have been placed there to assist the departed in their journey — I truly think that other items were simply momentos of the journey the deceased completed here in this world. Some knapping tools left beside a knapper, a favorite knife, a cherished family heirloom pendant, etc.

So, were bannerstones made to be counter-balance weights used on atl-atls? Were they made to be totems or clan symbols to identify one's tribal affiliation? Were they status symbols for tribal elders or leaders or were they made as an ornate object to be placed in the graves of people of special stature? My feeling is that all of the above are probably true to some degree.

The reasons that brought me to this conclusion are several-fold. First, there are simply too many lower and mid-grade bannerstones that have been found with evidence of wear and use to claim they were never used. Second and at the opposite end of the scale, are similarly shaped but much more ornate examples that would never hold up to the stress of actual use. Third is the finding of ornately designed bannerstones situated with remnants of other atl-atl component parts such as hooks and handles that were, for whatever unknown reasons, sometimes place in graves with the deceased.

Let's think logically for a second about what we do know about bannerstones as utilitarian tools, then we can think about them as ceremonial objects.

Not all bannerstones are the same size and style, and thus it is probable that the variance in

styles may indicate that while they are basically made for the same general purpose, some designs such as the fluted ball and the tube banners were made for use, while others such as notched ovates and knobbed crescents were made for ceremonial or mortuary purposes. It would be the same as what we do with guns in modern times. I have a nice .54 caliber black powder rifle I love to deer hunt with, while I also have a beautifully inlaid presentation rifle of the same caliber. One I take into the woods and hunt with, the other hangs on the wall in my office and will be passed down to my son one day for his wall. Both are guns — but one is made in an elaborate fashion strictly for appearance. The one I hunt with has scratches and nicks from daily use during deer season; the other is in mint condition and I oil it regularly even though it stays on the wall. I think the same may be true for bannerstones.

If an ornate banner was not placed on a staff to identify a clan or person of some special stature, then it could easily have been part of a presentation-grade atl-atl used for some unknown ceremony, ritual, designation, or award. There is really no way of knowing; but, mankind tends to do today many of the things we did in the past. Biggest buck winner in a hunting contest now often gets a new gun as a prize or a trophy. Was an elaborately designed atl-atl a trophy of sorts in ancient times? Who knows, again, we can only speculate, but there is no doubt that they did have a significance to the ancient ones who crafted them.

Pictured are some bannerstone styles that fall into the highly problematical category when trying to determine actual use and purpose in ancient times. It is hard to imagine these styles ever being used along with a functioning atl-atl system due to the size, style, and fragile nature of their design.

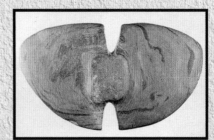

4⅝" notched wing bannerstone made from glacial slate. Complete except for perforation. Pictured in Who's Who #1. Mike Barron collection. $850.00

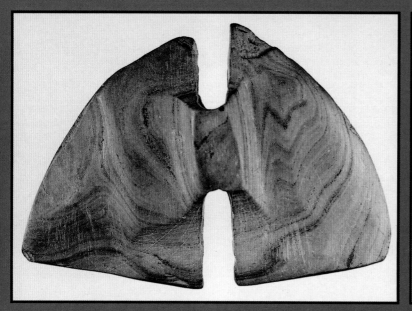

4½" notched butterfly bannerstone found in Marion Co., OH. Collection of Gene Edwards. $1,600.00

2¾" double notched wing bannerstone found in Ionia Co., MI. Ex. Spaulding. Collection Frank Otto. Museum Grade

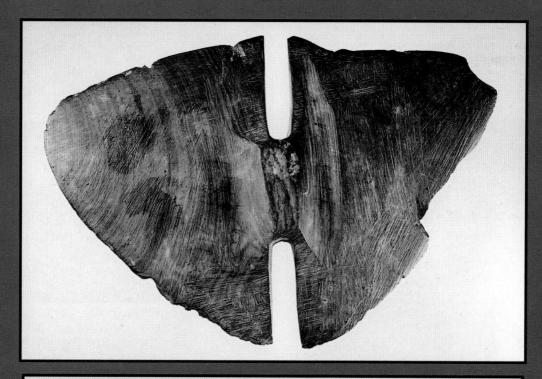

6⅜" double notched butterfly bannerstone found in Hardin Co., OH. Gene Edwards collection. $1,200.00

4½" winged bannerstone with a single notch. Found in Ashland Co., OH. Collection of Alan Selders. $1,000.00

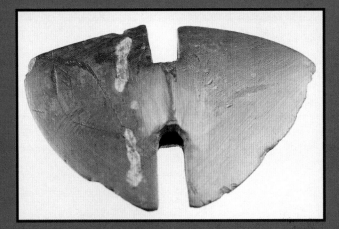

4¹⁵⁄₁₆" notched butterfly bannerstone found in Madison Co., OH. Collection of Doug Hooks. $1,500.00

5¼" salvaged knobbed lunate found in Ross Co., OH. Salvaged ends have been polished over. Collection of Doug Hooks. $750.00

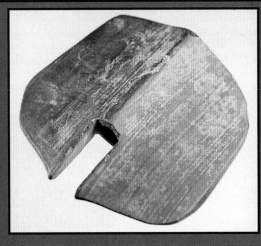

3½" single notched butterfly bannerstone that was salvaged from a larger broken bannerstone in ancient times. Found near Waverly, OH. Collection of Doug Hooks. $1,000.00

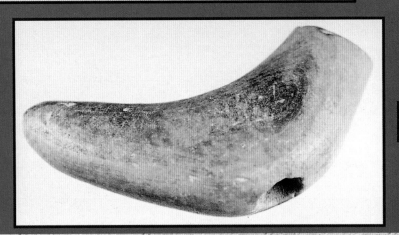

3⅝" salvaged lunate style bannerstone found in Hocking Co., OH. Collection of Doug Hooks. $300.00

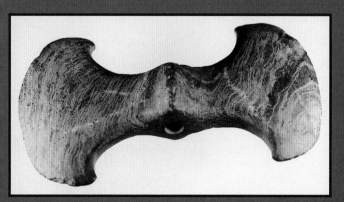

Exceptionally nice stylized double crescent bannerstone that measures 6⅝" long x 3¾" wide. Made from nicely banded slate, found near Salem, OH. Ex. Phillips, ex. Tolliver. Collection of Doug Hooks. Museum Grade

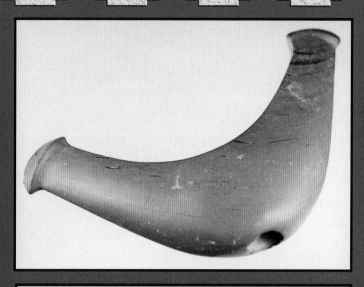

5⅜" wide knobbed lunate found near Toledo, OH. Ex. Johnson, ex. Fuller, ex. Tolliver. Collection of Doug Hooks. Museum Grade

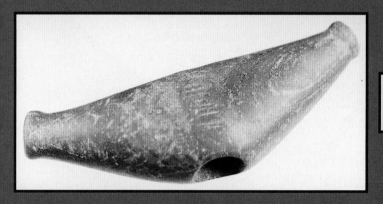

3¹⁵⁄₁₆" knobbed lunate found in Crawford Co., OH. This is a miniature size for this style bannerstone. This also represents that lunates are not all crescent shaped. Collection of Doug Hooks. $3,500.00

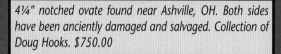

4¼" notched ovate found near Ashville, OH. Both sides have been anciently damaged and salvaged. Collection of Doug Hooks. $750.00

5" long double crescent found in Park Co., IN. Collection of Frank Otto. $1,800.00

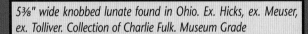

5⅜" wide knobbed lunate found in Ohio. Ex. Hicks, ex. Meuser, ex. Tolliver. Collection of Charlie Fulk. Museum Grade

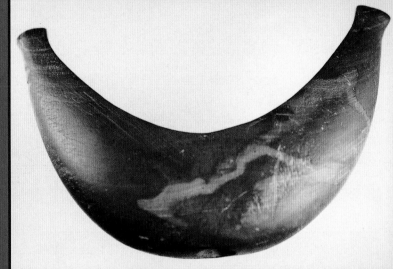

5⅛" long notched ovate found in Preble Co., OH. Ex. Wachtel, ex. Tolliver, ex. Meuser. Collection of Charlie Fulk. $1,300.00

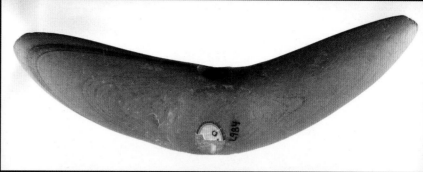

6" x 2½" crescent found in Ohio. Collection of Dennis Link. $5,000.00

Beautiful banded slate notched ovate. Very large at 5⅞" long. This style is from the east or Midwest. Ex. Tolliver collection. Currently in the collection of Doug Hooks. Museum Grade

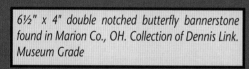

6½" x 4" double notched butterfly bannerstone found in Marion Co., OH. Collection of Dennis Link. Museum Grade

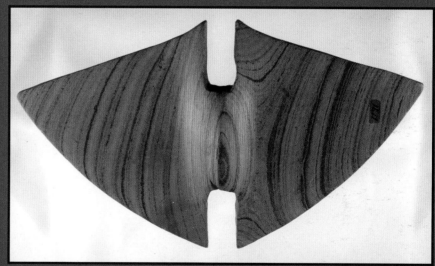

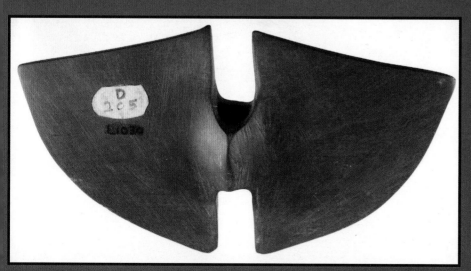

5⅛" x 3" double notched wing butterfly bannerstone found in OH. Ex. Trauterman. Collection of Dennis Link. $5,000.00

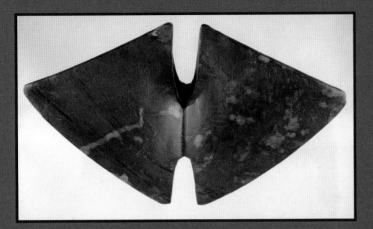

5¼" x 3¼" double notched wing butterfly bannerstone found in Ohio. Collection of Dennis Link. $5,000.00

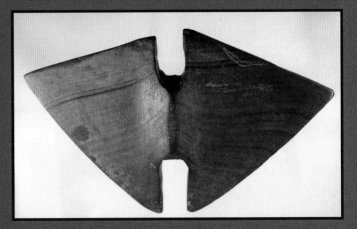

5¾" x 3½" double notched wing butterfly bannerstone found in Ohio. Collection of Dennis Link. $5,000.00

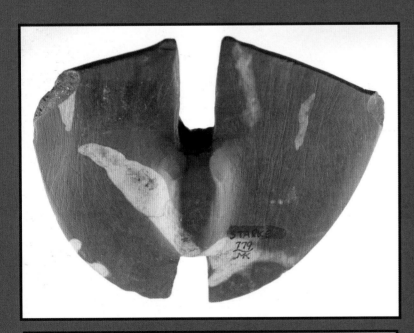

3⅝" x 3¼" double notched wing butterfly bannerstone found in Starke Co., OH. Eric Wagner collection. $1,500.00

Salvaged 3" x 2¼" double notched wing butterfly bannerstone found in Indiana. Courtesy of the Museum of Native American Artifacts. $650.00

4¾" long x 2½" tall double notch butterfly bannerstone found in Ohio. Ex. Marian Bush WW #2, page 33. Collection of John Dickinson. $2,000.00

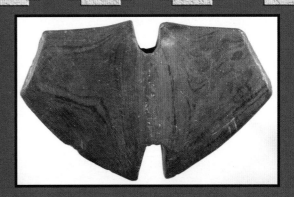

Salvaged 4⅜" long x 3" tall double notched wing butterfly bannerstone found near Willoughby, OH. Collection of John Dickinson. $750.00

One of the more interesting and rarer styles of the notched butterfly bannerstone group are the tie-on variety. These were made thinner than their perforated counterparts and lack the wider barrel in the middle where the drilling would have been placed.

5⅛" winged butterfly bannerstone. Rare undrilled tie-on style found in Berrien Co., MI. Ex. Townsend, ex. Spaulding. Collection of Frank Otto. Museum Grade

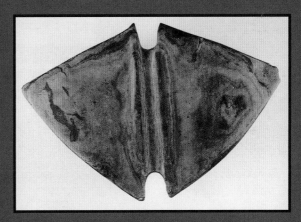

5½" x 3⅝" rare style grooved and notched butterfly winged bannerstone found in Michigan. Collection of Dave Yallup. Museum Grade

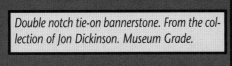

Double notch tie-on bannerstone. From the collection of Jon Dickinson. Museum Grade.

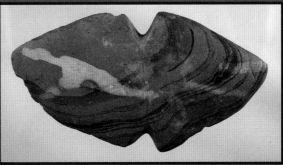

In addition to the many styles of perforated bannerstones, weights were also used that tied directly to the atl-atl shaft. Many of these styles of weights had a groove incised around their midsection or notches inserted for easier and more secure attachment. Listed are some of the tie-on weight styles that were used in ancient times:

Loafstones & Grooved Loafstones
Flat Weights
Bar Weights
Drilled Bar Weights
Bar Amulets
Elliptical Bar Weights
Tie-on Butterflys

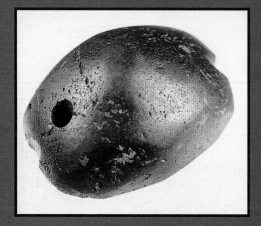

2³⁄₁₆" notched and drilled loafstone style atl-atl weight made from hematite. Found in Marion Co., TN. Ex. Pinkston. Courtesy of Back to Earth Rocks & Relics. $225.00

2³⁄₈" loafstone made from quartzite, found in Ashland Co., OH. Ex. Thornberg. Collection of Bob Bright. $250.00

2" long grooved weight found by Bob Bright in Ashland Co., OH. Collection of Bob Bright. Personal Find

2⁵⁄₈" long x 1³⁄₈" wide red slate loafstone found in Kentucky. Collection of Bob Bright. $275.00

2⅛" long grooved atl-atl weight found in Ashland Co., OH, by Bob Bright. Made from banded slate. Collection of Bob Bright. Personal Find

2" long grooved loafstone found in Kentucky. This loafstone is unique as it has two grooves going in opposite directions. Collection of Bob Bright. $175.00

2⅞" nicely polished loafstone found in Ashland Co., OH. Collection of Bob Bright. $225.00

2¼" long loafstone found in Ohio. Collection of Bob Bright. $175.00

2³⁄₁₆" hematite bar weight found in Wayne Co., OH. Ex. Wehrle. Don Casto collection. $100.00

Pair of loafstones made from hematite. Left is a cone shaped type from Illinois, $35.00; right is a loafstone style found in Ohio, $50.00; Lar Hothem collection.

1⅝" long loafstone made from granite, found in Clermont Co., OH. Collection of Fred Winegardner. $225.00

2⅜" loafstone made from granite, found in Franklin Co., OH. Collection of Fred Winegardner. $125.00

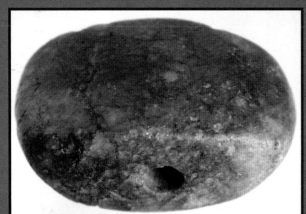

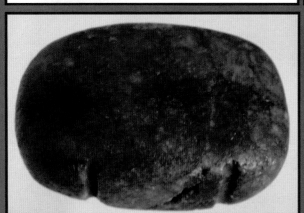

2¼" bannerstone partially drilled and then grooved for tie-on. Found in Medina County, Ohio. Gene Edwards collection. $75.00

1⅝" long loafstone made from hematite. Found in Coshocton Co., OH. Collection of Lar Hothem. $75.00

4" long ungrooved atl-atl weight made from sandstone, found near Greenfield, IN. Collection of Bob Bright. $325.00

4½" grooved bar weight found in Ohio. Collection of Bob Bright. $325.00

3¾" long grooved bar weight found in Franklin Co., OH. Collection of Bob Bright. $325.00

3¾" grooved bar weight made from green slate, found in Paulding Co., OH. Collection of Bob Bright. $325.00

4¾" pick-shaped bar weight, found in Ohio. Collection of Bob Bright. $250.00

4¾" bar weight found in Ohio. Collection of Bob Bright. $175.00

3¹⁄₁₆" hardstone atl-atl weight found in Richland Co., OH. Ex. Jack Hooks. Collection of Doug Hooks. $150.00

3¾" grooved atl-atl weight found in Knox Co., OH. Collection of Sam Speck. $400.00

6³⁄₁₆" bar weight found in Clermont Co., OH. Collection of Charlie Fulk. $350.00

5⅝" long elliptical bar weight that has been grooved at mid-section for attachment. Found in Ohio. Ex. Wehrle #2855W, ex. Hupp. Collection of Fred Winegardner. Museum Grade

2⅝" long bar weight found in Ohio. Collection of Fred Winegardner. $60.00

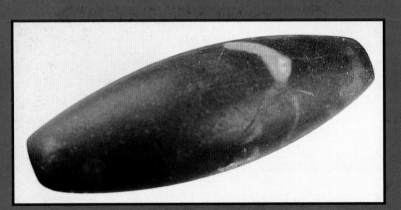

3½" bar weight found in Fairfield Co., OH. Collection of Fred Winegardner. $250.00

3¹⁄₁₆" bar weight found in Ross Co., OH. Collection of Fred Winegardner. $125.00

2⅞" bar weight made from hematite. Ends have been notched for attachment. Found in Scioto Co., OH. Collection of Fred Winegardner. $250.00

3¼" bar weight made from hardstone. Found in Ashland Co., OH. Collection of Charlie Fulk. $350.00

4¼" grooved bar weight found in Preble Co., OH. Collection of Charlie Fulk. $350.00

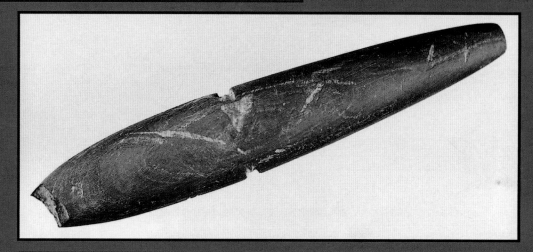

5⅜" grooved bar weight, Midwest style, damage to one end. Collection of Dave Yallup. $100.00

2¹¹⁄₁₆" bar weight found in Fairfield Co., OH. Collection of Lar Hothem. $75.00

2¹³⁄₁₆" bar weight found in Coshocton Co., OH. Collection of Lar Hothem. $250.00

3⅛" grooved bar weight found in Kentucky. Collection of Lar Hothem. $225.00

Notched atl-atl weight, unique style. Found in Huron Co., OH. Collection of Bob Bright. $150.00

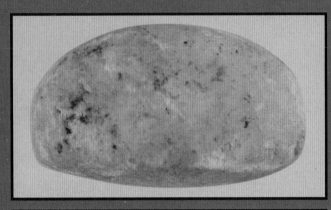

2" long grooved loafstone made from quartz. Found in Fayette Co., KY. Collection of Benny Webb. Personal Find

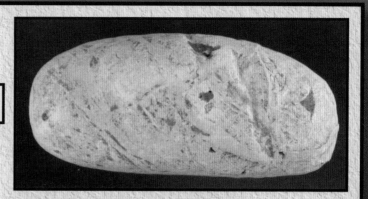

2" loafstone made from galena. Found in Fayette Co., KY. Collection of Benny Webb. Personal Find

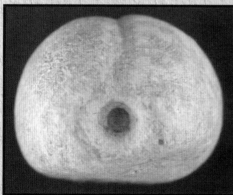

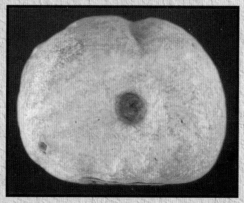

1¾" long loafstone made from galena. Found in Clark Co., KY. Collection of Benny Webb. Personal Find

2⅜" loafstone, hardstone, Madison Co., KY. Hayden Bybee collection. $125.00

2⅞" x 1¼" white quartz loafstone found in Madison Co., KY. Collection of David Denny. Personal Find

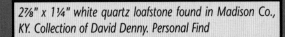

1⅞" loafstone made from galena. Collection of John Gibson. Personal Find

2½" loafstone made from hardstone. Collection of John Gibson. Personal Find

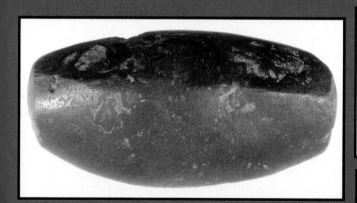

Hematite loafstone, 2½" long with a notched top. Found in Galia Co., OH. Collection of Jon Dickinson. $175.00

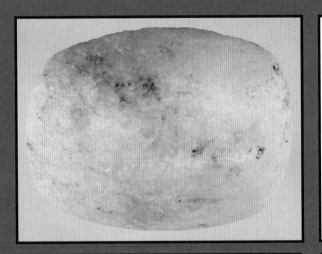

2⅛" loafstone made from quartz. Found in Bethel, OH. Collection of Jon Dickinson. $225.00

2⅛" grooved loaf found near Windster, OH. Collection of Jon Dickinson. $200.00

2¼" loafstone found in Montgomery Co., KY. Collection of Jon Dickinson. $185.00

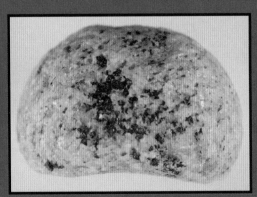

2⅛" loafstone made from garnet schist and found in Clement Co., OH. Collection of Jon Dickinson. Personal Find

Drilled bar weight/boatstone found in Jackson Co., OH. Ex. C. Smith. Collection of Jon Dickinson. $500.00

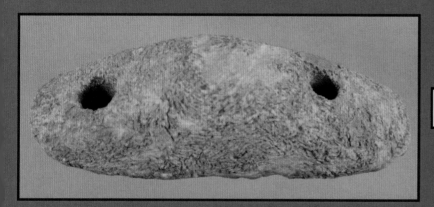

2⅝" drilled galena loafstone found in Woodford Co., KY. Collection of Jon Dickinson. $250.00

Galena loafstone found in Highland Co., OH. Collection of Jon Dickinson. $250.00

3" weight with nice incised line detail. Found in Macklenberg Co., VA. Maxey collection, Courtesy of Cliff Jackson. Museum Grade

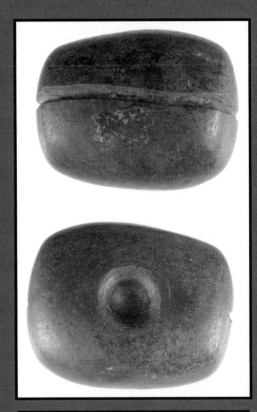

2⅛" x 1⅛" loafstone made from siltstone. Found in north Alabama. Charles Ray collection. $85.00

2" x 1½" loafstone made from siltstone found in south Alabama. Charles Ray collection. $125.00

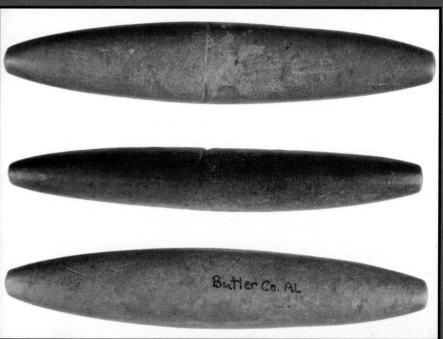

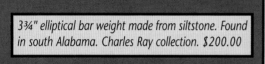
3¾" elliptical bar weight made from siltstone. Found in south Alabama. Charles Ray collection. $200.00

Unique 2¾" grooved slate weight found in Ohio. Gene Edwards collection. $75.00

3¼" notched and tallied weight made from banded slate. Found in Ohio. Colelction of Gene Edwards. $275.00

5⅛" tie-on weight found in Ohio. Unique style, could be classified as a slate lizard. Collection of Lar Hothem. Restored

5½" bar weight found in Central Ohio. Ex. Cline. Collection of Lar Hothem. $375.00

2¾" hematite bar weight found in Fairfield Co., Ohio. Collection of Lar Hothem. $45.00

5⅛" bar weight found in Central Ohio. Ex. Cline. Collection of Lar Hothem. $375.00

3" bar loaf found in Clement, OH. Jon Dickinson collection. $175.00

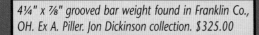

4¼" x ⅞" grooved bar weight found in Franklin Co., OH. Ex A. Piller. Jon Dickinson collection. $325.00

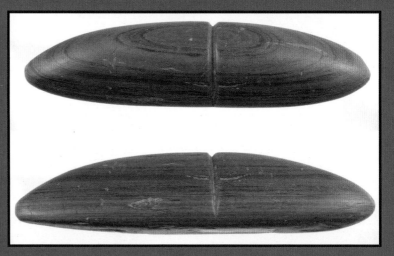

2⅛" x 1⁹⁄₁₆" grooved hollow loafstone with engraving. Found in Kentucky. Collection of Tom Davis. $150.00

Slate lizard, 3" long, Garrard Co., KY. Found by David Friley. Many of what collectors call lizards were most likely stylized tie-on weights, such as this example. Randal Carrier collection. Museum Grade

2" x 1⅜" x ¾" wide hemisphere. Hemispheres are like loafstones, only thinner in cross-section. These were also used as tie-on weights. Collection of Tom Davis. $250.00

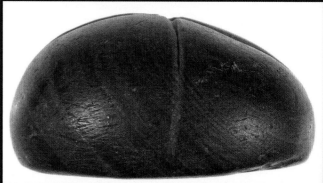

2¼" x 1½" x 1" tall loafstone with unique double groove. Found in Ohio. Collection of Tom Davis. $250.00

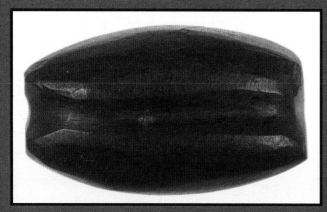

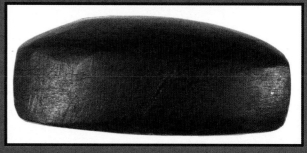

2" x 1⅛" x ⅞" tall grooved weight found in Ohio. Collection of Tom Davis. $175.00

1⅞" x 1⅜" x ⅞" tall loafstone made from galina. Found in Kentucky. Collection of Tom Davis. $150.00

2⅜" notched atl-atl weight found in Ohio. Ex. Snyder. Collection of Bob Bright. $150.00

Boatstones & Bar Amulets

Believed to be types of tie-on weights, boatstones are elongated in style and often have two drill holes placed in either the midsection or the ends for attachment. The bottoms on most examples of boatstones have been scooped out. Bar amulets are similar as they also were crafted with an elongated shape, and have two holes for attachment but have a flat botom. The difference in drilling between the two are the holes on amulets are placed on the bottom ends rather than from the top down. Bar amulets also have an easy to identify shape as the ends taper in an upward direction. There is no clear documented connection that I found while researching this book between the boatstone and bar amulet to the atl-atl; however, I feel the assumption is made based on the similarity of the style of this artifact type when compared to other tie-on atl-atl weight styles.

4⅞" boatstone found in Allen Co., IN. Photo shows the scooped-out bottom common on most boatstones. Gene Edwards collection. $450.00

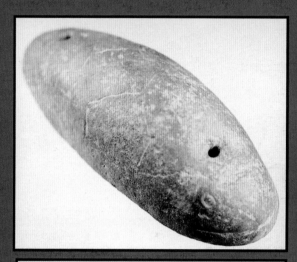

4⅝" long drilled boatstone found near Perrysville, OH. This is a rare effigy style. Collection of Sam Speck. Museum Grade

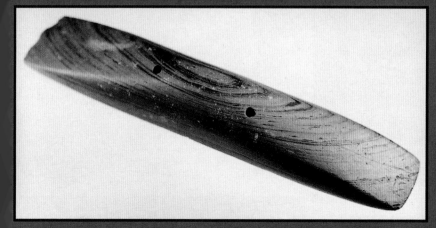

6" drilled boatstone found in Ashland Co., OH. Ex. Bob Bright. Collection of Charlie Fulk. $1,300.00

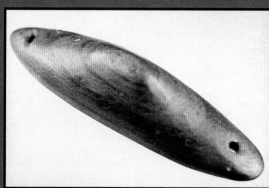

3⅝" boatstone found in Holmes Co., OH. Drilled on both ends. Collection Sam Speck. $1,000.00

3⅛" long drilled boatstone made from galena. Found in Kentucky. Collection of Chris Smith. $400.00

4³⁄₁₆" bar amulet drilled at both ends. Found in Montgomery Co., OH. Collection of Chris Smith. $600.00

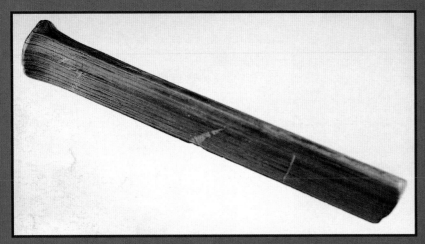

5½" bar amulet found in Miami Co., OH. Drilled on both ends. Ex. Walls, ex. Hawks. Collection of Charlie Fulk. Museum Grade

3⅜" drilled bar amulet found in Preble Co., OH. Ex. Andy Parks. Doug Hooks collection. $350.00

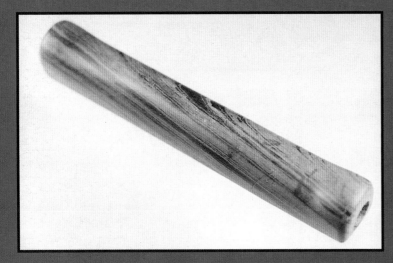

4¼" drilled bar amulet found in Warren Co., OH. Collection of Charlie Fulk. $650.00

5" long drilled bar amulet found in Vinton Co., OH. Ex. Saunders. Collection of Doug Hooks. $1,200.00

Miniature Bannerstones

One of the more intriguing anomalies of the various groups of ancient artifacts is the presence of miniature examples that have been recovered over the years. From miniature celts and axes to micro-sized flint points, the creation of miniatures can be found in many artifact groups, bannerstones included. The famous Mueser collection contained a variety of excellent examples of miniature bannerstones, and I was fortunate to have been able to view many of these Mueser miniatures that had been assembled by Ohio collector Mike Barron. The purpose behind the creation of miniatures in ancient times remains one of the many mysteries that surround bannerstones as a whole. While theories ranging from miniatures having a ceremonial significance to simply being child's toys abound, there is no documented evidence suggesting what the specific reason was behind their manufacture, or what specific role they played in the lives of our ancient American forefathers. The finding of miniature sized bannerstones in an archaeological context as well as in documented surface finds tells us only that these items existed in ancient times, leaving us to extrapolate our own theories as to their ancient crafters reason for their manufacture. The majority of miniature bannerstones recovered to date are often near to exact scale, and very well made. As collectors and students of ancient America, it is often hard, yet unfortunately necessary, to accept the fact that for now, some things, as in the case of miniature bannerstones, will have to remain a mystery, leaving us to wait patiently until new evidence is discovered. Until some future archaeological excavation uncovers such artifacts in an insitu context, we must content ourselves to enjoy the artifacts themselves for their uniqueness and craftsmanship as we ponder the reasons behind their existence.

1¾" wide miniature winged bannerstone found in Ohio. Ex. Dick Johnson. Collection of Fred Winegardner. $650.00

1¼" wide miniature ball bannerstone found in Ashland Co., Ohio by Bob Bright in 1990. Collection of Bob Bright. Personal Find

1¾" miniature tube bannerstone found in northern Ohio. Collection of Fred Winegardner. $300.00

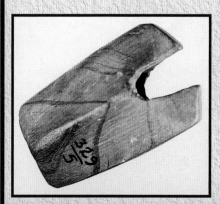

2⅜" miniature single notched winged bannerstone that has been salvaged in ancient times. Found in Richland Co., OH. Collection of Fred Winegardner. Museum Grade

2⅛" miniature winged bannerstone found in Ohio. Ex. Sam Speck. Collection of Fred Winegardner. $350.00

One of the most interesting traits found on some bannerstones is the solid physical evidence indicating that after being damaged in ancient times, they were then subjected to a variety of repair methods. One can only surmise that repairing or salvaging damaged bannerstones was done so as to prolong their usefulness. Although the exact manner of that continued use may be subject to discussion, the fact that they were repaired rather than discarded leads one to wonder why such efforts were made in ancient times to see to their continued use. On one hand it can be argued that repairs were made simply as a matter of efficiency as to repair a bannerstone took much less time than to craft a new one from scratch. On the other hand, it can be argued that bannerstones may have been thought to have some mystical or supernatural association or possibly some additional sentimental value as heirlooms, and thus it was important on that level to not discard them. Either way, they were often salvaged, and thus returned to use by their ancient owners, whatever that use may have been.

When you consider from a logical standpoint how the component parts of an atl-atl would be assembled, a perforated bannerstone would have to be fitted onto the atl-atl shaft before the hook and handle were both attached. Once together, there would be no easy way to place a new bannerstone over the hook or handle should the original banner break away from the shaft. Rather than removing either the hook, or the handle, both of which would have been hafted most likely with some form of natural adhesive, other techniques were developed to repair the weapon. Since most times the bannerstones would break in the middle at the hole, it would make logical sense that taking those two damaged pieces and tying them together around the atl-atl shaft would be the most efficient way to correct the damage.

So why salvage the original bannerstone in this fashion rather than just tying on a different style tie-on weight? I think there are several factors here to consider, the first being that it would be most efficient to recycle the parts that are already available. Secondly, in the matter of a utilitarian working atl-atl, it was a matter of matching the weight exactly to what the thrower was used to. All weapons have traits that their user learns and grows accustomed to. My favorite rifle for varmit hunting is a .223 with a very sensitive trigger. I like a sensitive trigger when taking long shots with the use of a scope, and I know when I have the target bracketed in my scope exactly how much pressure for my finger to apply when I am ready to take the shot. I have used this particular gun for over a decade, and if I were to adjust the trigger pull, it would affect my accuracy until I grew accustomed to the change. If an ancient hunter used an atl-atl for any length of time, he would know exactly how much force to apply to his throws to obtain different distances accurately. If he were to change the weight of his counter balance, it would likely affect how the weapon handled, and thus affect the accuracy of his throws, just as adjusting the trigger on my rifle would affect my shot. That, I feel, is one reason so many weights were salvaged.

Thirdly, let us assume the bannerstone in question was ceremonial in nature, not utilitarian. It would not be hard to draw the conclusion that breaking a sacred object or heirloom would necessitate repairing it.

No matter what the reason for repairing broken bannerstones, the fact is clearly documented by the salvaged artifacts left behind that it was a common practice in ancient times.

The most common repairs I have seen are done to the winged variety of bannerstones. When broken at the center hole that fits over the shaft, a single small hole, or multiple small holes would be placed into each half so that it could be fitted over the shaft and tied back together again.

5⅛" winged bannerstone made from slate and found in Indiana. Banner halves were found one year apart. One piece found in 1999 and the other in 2000. Hayden Bybee collection. $200.00

Examples of salvaged banners with drilled repairs holes:

Salvaged bannerstone found in Indiana. Collection of David & Aaron Kilander. $100.00

Salvaged slate found in Indiana. Collection of David & Aaron Kilander. $100.00

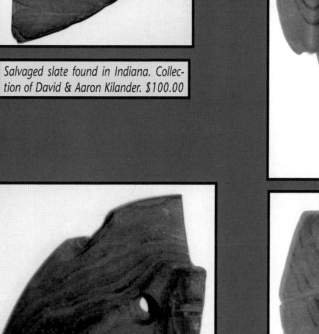

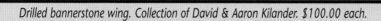

Drilled bannerstone wing. Collection of David & Aaron Kilander. $100.00 each.

Salvaged winged bannerstone found in Indiana.

3¾" salvaged winged bannerstone with multiple drill holes, found in Ohio. Collection Frank Otto. $250.00 due to uniqueness

3¾" salvaged winged bannerstone with multiple drill holes, found in Ohio. Collection Frank Otto. $250.00 due to uniqueness

3" salvaged bannerstone wing made from Chlorite, eastern United States style. The size of the perforation hole indicates this was salvaged into a pendant. Collection Frank Otto. Price Unlisted

Bannerstone, 1¾" x 1½", siltstone, south Georgia, salvaged. Charles Ray collection. $200.00

Bannerstone 1⅝" x 1⅝", siltstone, south Alabama, with grooves. Charles Ray collection. $50.00

Bannerstone that was broken and repaired in ancient times. Collection of Lar Hothem. $50.00

Two wing bannerstone with salvage holes, 4½" and 3¾". Found in Ohio. Lar Hothem collection.

On other styles of bannerstones repairs were made by incising a groove or notches or both on the damaged parts to help tie them together.

Examples of salvaged banners with incised grooves and notches:

1½" x 1½" bannerstone made from siltstone that broke in half, and one side was then grooved to be used as a tie-on weight. Found in south Alabama. Collection of Charles Ray. $85.00

1¾" x 1½" bannerstone half that was grooved along one edge so that it could be used as a tie-on weight. Made from siltstone and found in south Alabama. Collection of Charles Ray. $85.00

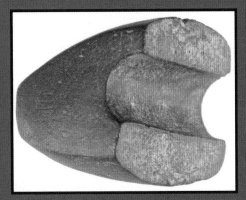
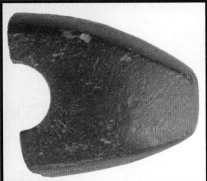
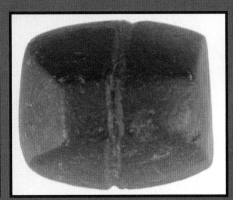

1¼" x 1⅛" bannerstone that broke and one end was grooved and then used as a tie-on weight. Made from siltstone and found in south Alabama. Collection of Charles Ray. $85.00

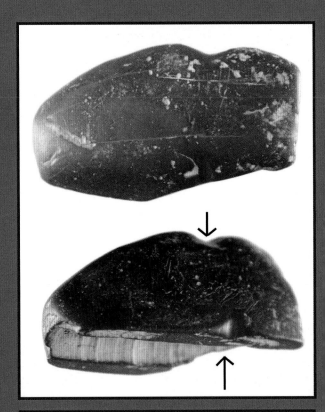

3¼" salvaged fluted tube bannerstone found in Indiana. Broken in half lengthwise at the hole, then grooved around midsection to be used as a tie-on weight. Lar Hothem collection. $125.00

Bannerstone half that was notched after breakage so that it could be used as a tie-on weight. Made from black steatite and found in Halifax Co., NC. Cliff Jackson collection. $85.00

Not all bannerstones broke at the hole. Many times, especially on the winged style of banners, the wing area would become damaged and would require reattachment. Multiple holes would be drilled on both sides of the break allowing the pieces to be tied back together.

Notched wing butterfly bannerstone found in Indiana that shows where part of one wing was drilled for salvage. David & Aaron Kilander collection. $350.00

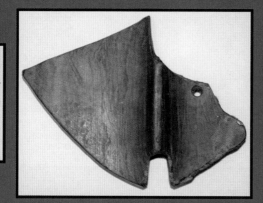

Notched wing bannerstone found in Indiana that shows where part of one wing was drilled for salvage. David & Aaron Kilander collection. $450.00

One other form of salvaging that was done on pick style banners that had broken at the hole was to place a new hole into the broken sections not for the purpose of tying the two broken pieces back together, but rather to make one or possibly two new bannestones from the damaged halves. As we previously discussed, there would have been no easy way to slide these newly perforated banners back over the atl-atl shaft as the hook and handle would still be in place, so one can assume that this style salvaged banner would probably be used on a newly crafted atl-atl.

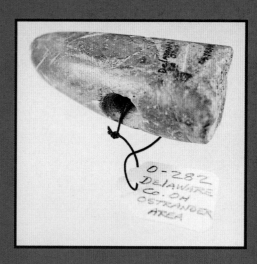

2⅛6" salvaged pick bannerstone made from chlorite with secondary drilled hole. Found in Delaware Co., OH. Collection Frank Otto. $275.00

2⅛" salvaged pick bannerstone made from chlorite with secondary drilled hole. Found in Delaware Co., OH. Ex. Dick Coulter. Collection Frank Otto. $250.00

Salvaged Bannerstones

Another thought with regard to this style of salvaging is trying to determine when the damage occurred. Quite possibly with this type of salvage, the damaged halves broke during the drilling process and were never previously attached to an atl-atl, so a new hole was simply added next to where the original hole had been started. As you can see in the example to the right, the original drilling to this particular salvaged pick was never completed. It broke while being drilled as the original hole never perforated the opposite side of the banner.

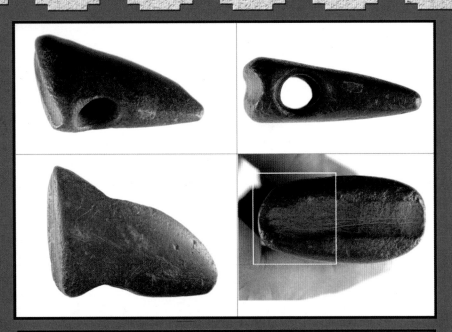

2½" winged bannerstone that had remaining wing adjusted and a new hole drilled for attachement. Found in North Carolina. Collection of Cliff Jackson. $250.00

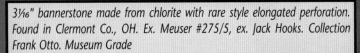

Another type of salvaging that is commonly seen on bannerstones is the shortening or "balancing" of the wings. If for some reason the pieces of the broken banner wing could not be reattached with ease, but the remainder of banner was still attached to the shaft, often the opposite wing size would be reduced to match the broken wing, thus balancing out the weight. See below example.

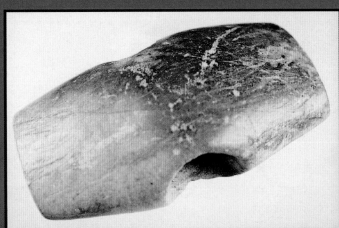

3¹⁄₁₆" bannerstone made from chlorite with rare style elongated perforation. Found in Clermont Co., OH. Ex. Meuser #275/5, ex. Jack Hooks. Collection Frank Otto. Museum Grade

Evidence I found while examining artifacts for this book indicates that some bannerstones, both completed as well as salvaged, were in fact used as ornamentation. While no reason as to why certain bannerstones and bannerstone pieces were selected over others can be determined with any degree of certainty, the fact remains that some examples clearly indicate ornamental use, whether for ceremonial purposes, or simple personal decoration.

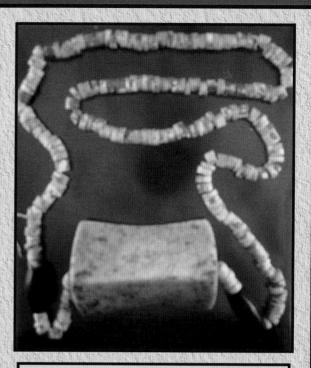

Bannerstone found in Ohio Co., Kentucky, in the 1930s in a burial site at the Indian Knoll site. Found with a necklace in a grave laying on top of the skeletal remains. Found together as part of a necklace with shell beads and two canal coal beads. Collection of Charlie Wagers. Museum Grade

Two hole pendant/gorget made from the broken wing of a butterfly bannerstone. Collection of David & Aaron Kilander. $250.00

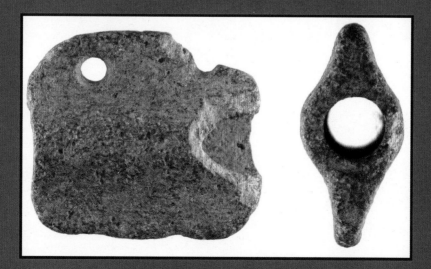

Salvaged bannerstone that later had a suspension hole drilled along one edge. Cliff Jackson collection. $200.00

Surface Etching on Damaged Slate Artifacts

To add another layer of intrigue to the bannerstone group as well as to the flat slate artifacts groups such as pendants and gorgets is the fact that many broken and salvaged slate artifacts had unique etching placed into their surfaces. While not all slate artifacts that have been broken have incised line etchings on them, the majority of etchings I have seen have been placed on slate artifacts after they had broke. Whether these etchings were placed on the damaged items because of some spiritual belief or to ward off potential additional bad luck or not, it does add an additional level of intrigue to such items.

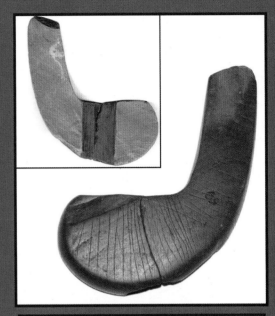

3½" salvaged geniculate found near Canton, Stark Co., Ohio. Highly engraved with straight incised lines. Collection of Rob Dills. $275.00

Broken bannerstone which has had incised lines placed inside the broken hole area in ancient times. Collection of Lar Hothem. $85.00

3½" bannerstone made from siltstone and found in south Alabama. After breakage, this piece was notched for reattachement and incised lines were placed around the notch. Charles Ray collection. $40.00

Pecked and ground stone tools, weapons, and ornaments first begin to show up in the archaeological record in North America during the Archaic period over 8,000 years ago. Axes and celts, pestles, pipes, and ornamental objects made from hardstone and slate were manufactured in large numbers during the Archaic. While ancient man was making pestles for grinding and axes and celts for chopping from stone, he was also beginning to fashion ornamental objects from slate and hardstone such as pendants and gorgets which had small drilled holes to allow the objects to be suspended around the neck or attached to his clothing. Many such ornaments when excavated have been found laying on top of the chest area of skeletal remains lending credence to the idea that perforated flat slate and hardstone pendants and gorgets were in fact worn as a form of ornamentation. The shape, size, and taper of the holes found in such ornamental objects indicates these perforations were made with the use of drills, most likely crafted from flint. Some examples of perforated flat slate and hardstone ornaments were drilled from only one side, while others had holes drilled from both sides. Unlike these flat stone items that were made for ornamentation, bannerstones needed a hole that was large enough to allow it to fit over the shaft of an atl-atl or staff, and this often required a different drilling technique. I say often because contrary to some beliefs on bannerstone production, I have seen and handled, on several occasions, examples of partially drilled bannerstones with smaller tapered holes which clearly

Small winged bannerstone that broke during the drilling process as evidenced by the fact that the drill hole was never completed. Found by Gary Henry in Buncombe Co., NC – April, 2006. Study Value

indicates a flint drill was in fact used, and others without the center core found from reed drilled examples indicating they may have been drilled with hardwood rods or other similar drilling techniques. While I have seen more than one example of a bannerstone that was partially drilled with a flint drill, the majority were drilled using a process known as "reed drilling." A hollow reed would be spun on the surface of the stone with the use of some abrasive material such as sand, which would then slowly cut a circular hole into the stone. In the center of the hole would be a core left from the hollow center portion of the reed. The fact that many partially drilled bannerstones have been found with a center core still in tact inside the hole is evidence that the reed drilling process was employed for drilling larger holes.

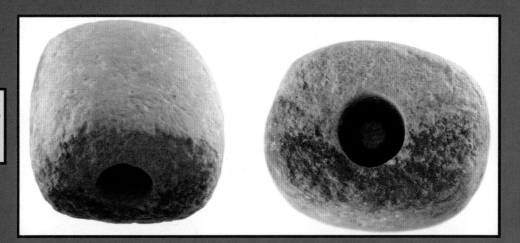

Partially drilled bannerstone preform with a clearly visible core left from the reed drilling process. Collection of John McCurdy. $75.00

Broken sections of reed drilled tube bannerstones. Note the closely spaced pattern left from the reed drilling process. Collection of Charles Ray. $5.00 – 10.00 each

Bannerstone preform showing evidence of reed drilling. Courtesy of Back to Earth Rocks & Relics. $75.00

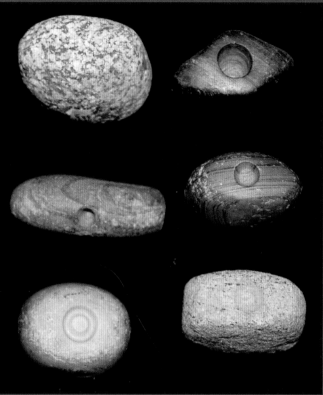

Set of six partially drilled bannerstone preforms. Jon Dickinson collection. $30.00 – 75.00 each

I have heard it theorized that possibly hollow bone may also have been used to drill such holes. I find this theory credible as bone being a denser material than reed would likely last longer during the drilling process, was readily available, and the hole size would fit the diameter of many of the bones found in small game and larger fowl. The abrasive that was used to cut into the stone could easily have been any mixture of material, but the use of sand or a sand and fat paste mixture would seem to make the most sense. Studies done long ago have shown that to completely make a bannerstone from start to finish could take as long as 180 hours, depending on how elaborate the design of the banner-stone was.

On many bannerstones made from banded glacial slate, the ancient crafter would position the banding on the slate so that the swirled pattern would be located on the barrel section in the center of the item. Many people have speculated that this was done purely for artistic rea-sons, making the complete banner more aesthetically

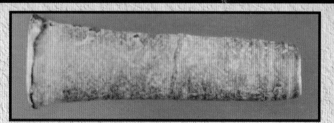

1⅛" bannerstone core found in crib mound in Spencer Co., Indiana. This is the core that was left after the hole was completed by reed drilling. This is a rare find. Collection of Charie Wagers. $200.00

pleasing. While this may in fact be true, there is another possible reason the swirled area was placed in the center.

When studying the grain patterns of slate used on bannerstones, I couldn't help but think back to my years of cabinet making. When working wood, one becomes familiar with the nature of the wood grain and how each area of the wood will react to being shaped, as well as how it will react to an outside force. Anyone who has worked with wood knows that a very straight grain when perforated is more likely to split, while wood with a swirled grain pattern is less likely to split. The burled area in a section of wood is the strongest part. Anyone who has ever split a piece of firewood knows that the straight grain pieces splits with ease, but when you come to a piece with a knotted section where the swirled grain is, it is much harder to separate the wood into two pieces. I think it is quite possible that ancient crafters found the same dynamics true with slate. Placing a hole through a straight grained section of the stone would be more prone to breakage during manufacture as well as during use than if a hole was placed through a swirled grain pattern of the stone. While it is true that having a swirled grain on the barrel of a bannersone makes the item more artistically beautiful, I am not convinced this placement of the grain pattern was done purely for artistic reasons. If I were going to spend 180 hours making an item, I would study the material closely to minimize the chance of breakage during manufacture, and to ensure it would last as long as possible once finished.

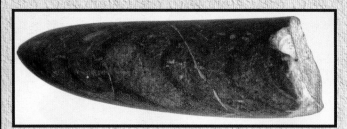

Bannerstone that broke shortly after the drilling process had begun. Gene Edward Collection. $25.00

Once the material for the bannerstone was chosen, the process of turning that raw material into a completed item would begin with reducing the raw material down to an oversized shape of what the final style would be. If the bannerstone was being made from a hardstone material, the ancient crafter would strike the surface of the stone with another smaller stone known as a hammerstone, removing small pieces of the material until this "pecking" process had reduced the stone to near its desired shape. Once this pecking process was completed, a hole would be drilled, and the surface of the relic would then be ground or sanded smooth.

In the case of a bannerstone being made from slate, the ancient crafter would strike the sides of the slate

material with the hammerstone removing large flakes of slate to reduce the material more quickly. Once the slate was thinned and somewhat shaped, he would then revert to the pecking process to continue the reduction of the material. Once the initial outside shape was roughed out, adjustments to correct the thickness of the piece would begin, leaving the bannerstone thicker in the center or "barrel" section for later drilling.

Bannerstone blank or preform that has been thinned, leaving a distinct barrel area for later drilling. Collection of Gene Edwards. $75.00

Bannerstone blank or preform that has been thinned, leaving a distinct barrel area for later drilling. Collection of Gene Edwards. $75.00

In the case of notched syle bannerstones such as ovates, a rare and very stylized form of bannerstone, the slate material was flaked and then pecked to a general oval shape, and then two circular holes were pecked completely through the material at opposite ends. Once the holes were completed, the crafter would peck and then cut away the outermost section of the hole to open the hole so as to allow access to the center barrel area for drilling.

In the case of smaller notches, often no drilling was necessary, and the stone material would be removed by cutting and gouging.

Once the shaping and drilling was completed, the exterior surfaces would be polished with an abrasive until smooth.

Examples of preform and partially drilled bannestones

4⅝" tube bannerstone preform with unique incised lines on top surface, drilling had not yet started. Found in Franklin Co., OH. Ex. Muser #292/5. Courtesy G. Thrush collection. $125.00

4⅛" rare style bannerstone found in southern Indiana, drill hole started on both sides. Collection of Gene Edwards. $350.00

3½" slate bannerstone preform found near Nashville, TN. Collection of Gene Edwards. $175.00

6" wide single notch butterfly bannerstone preform found in Ohio. Collection of Gene Edwards. $200.00

3" bannerstone preform that shows the original pecking on the surface. Found in Wabash Co., IN. Collection of Gene Edwards. $150.00

3⅝" bannerstone preform, Midwest style. Collection of Gene Edwards. $200.00

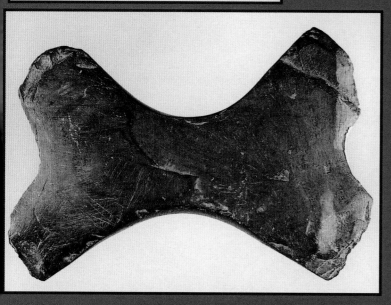

5⅛" bannerstone preform found in Ohio. Collection of Gene Edwards. $200.00

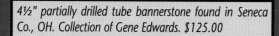

4½" partially drilled tube bannerstone found in Seneca Co., OH. Collection of Gene Edwards. $125.00

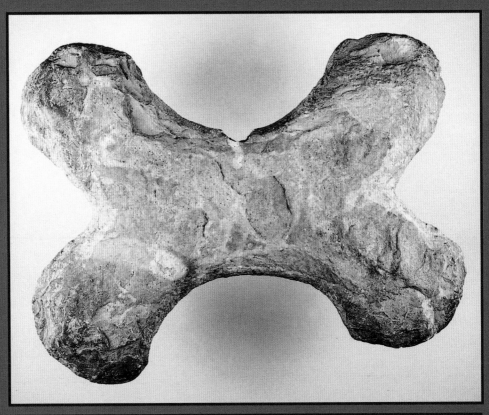

7¾" x 5½" bannerstone preform found in Indiana. Collection of Gene Edwards. $250.00

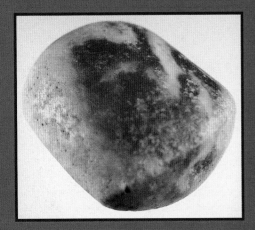

2⅝" bannerstone preform made from rose quartz. Collection of Gene Edwards. $300.00

2¾" x 2½" bannerstone preform made from gneiss. Found in Pickaway Co., OH. Collection of Lar Hothem. $100.00

2¾" long bannerstone preform which has been shaped but not drilled or polished. Found in southern Indiana. Collection of Lar Hothem. $175.00

3¼" tube bannerstone preform found in Franklin Co., OH. Don Casto collection. $100.00

4¾" winged bannerstone preform found in Ohio. Ex. Vietzen. Gene Edwards collection. $250.00

2½" wide unfinished bannerstone which is partially drilled. Made from limonite which has partially exfoliated. Found in Dyer Co., TN. Courtesy of Back to Earth Rocks & Relics. $80.00

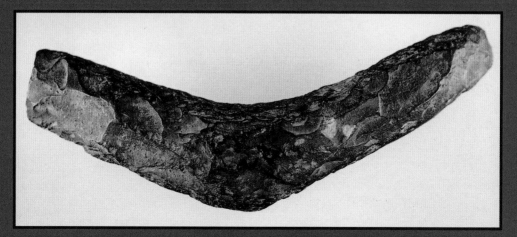

8⅛" crescent bannerstone found near Defiance, OH. Exterior surface shows rough first stage shaping. Gene Edwards collection. $150.00

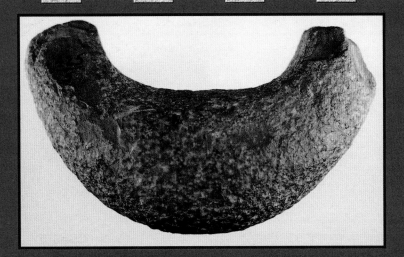

4⅞" crescent bannerstone preform. Exterior surface completed, however hole perforation had just begun. Found in Sandusky Co., OH. Gene Edwards collection. $300.00

5¼" crescent bannerstone preform found in Williams Co., OH. Surface shows original pecking. Ex. Meuser #425/5. Gene Edwards collection. $150.00

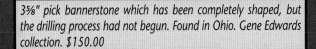

3⅝" pick bannerstone which has been completely shaped, but the drilling process had not begun. Found in Ohio. Gene Edwards collection. $150.00

10" crescent preform which has been shaped but not drilled. Midwest origin. Gene Edwards collection. $500.00

3¼" geniculate preform found in Union Co., OH. Gene Edwards collection. $150.00

4¾" winged bannerstone preform that has been partially drilled, found in Ohio. The exterior surface shows original pecking as final polishing had not begun. Gene Edwards collection. $200.00

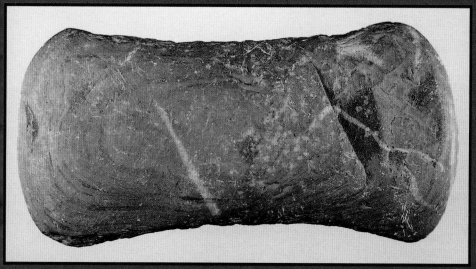

5¼" double bitted axe bannerstone preform found in Ohio. Gene Edwards collection. $100.00

3¾" reel bannerstone preform which has been pecked into shape but no drilling begun. Found in Mercer Co., OH. Gene Edwards collection. $150.00

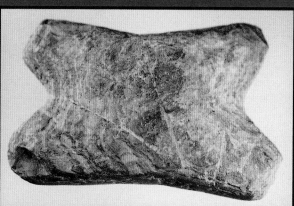

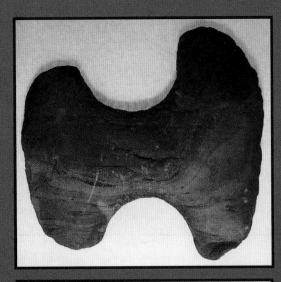

Slate bannerstone preform. Courtesy of Back to Earth Rocks & Relics. $150.00

4¹⁄₁₆" winged bannerstone preform made from translucent quartz. Found in southern Indiana. Collection of Alan Selders. Price Unlisted.

9¼" x 8" preform double crescent found in Indiana. David & Aaron Kilander collection. $150.00

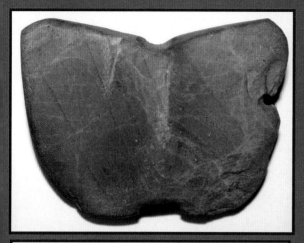

Drilled winged bannerstone preform found in Indiana. David & Aaron Kilander collection. $150.00

Drilled bannerstone preform found in Indiana. David & Aaron Kilander collection. $75.00

6¼" preform bannerstone found in Indiana. David & Aaron Kilander collection. $25.00

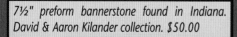

7½" preform bannerstone found in Indiana. David & Aaron Kilander collection. $50.00

6" preform bannerstone found in Indiana. David & Aaron Kilander collection. $35.00

Giniculate preform found in Indiana. David & Aaron Kilander collection. $50.00

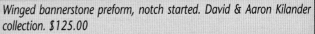

Winged bannerstone preform, notch started. David & Aaron Kilander collection. $125.00

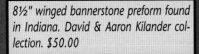

8½" winged bannerstone preform found in Indiana. David & Aaron Kilander collection. $50.00

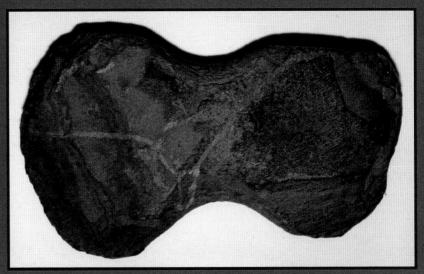

2¾" bannerstone perform. David & Aaron Kilander collection. $35.00

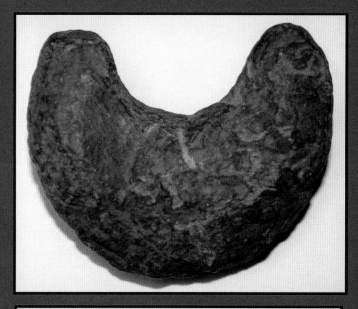

3" pick or crescent preform. David & Aaron Kilander collection. $125.00

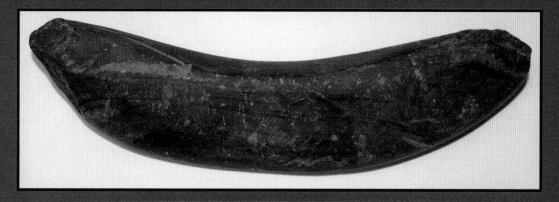

7" pick bannerstone perform. David & Aaron Kilander collection. $75.00

4" banner preform found in Warren Co., NC. Cliff Jackson collection. $75.00

3¾" banner preform found in Warren Co., NC. Cliff Jackson collection. $50.00

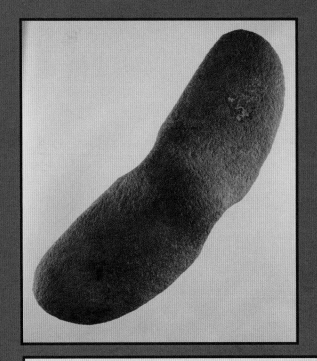

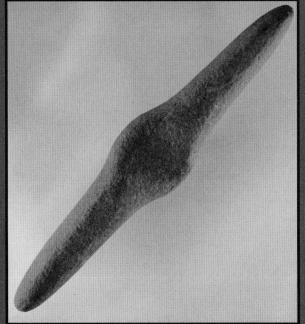

3⅝" banner preform found in Warren Co., NC. Cliff Jackson collection. $200.00

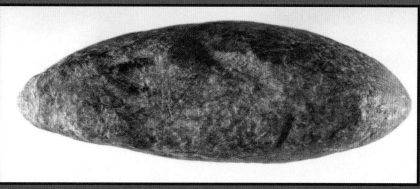

6¾" banner preform found in Warren Co., NC. Cliff Jackson collection. $50.00

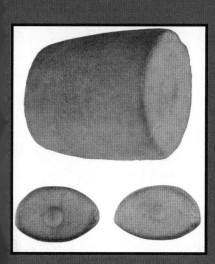

1¾" x 1" bannerstone preform made from sandstone. Found in south Alabama. Drilling started both ends. Charles Ray collection. $85.00

2½" x 2¼" Benton culture bannerstone preform made from siltstone. Found in south Alabama. Charles Ray collection. $100.00

3" bannerstone preform made from siltstone. Found in south Alabama. Charles Ray collection. $40.00

3" long bannerstone preform made from siltstone. Found in south Alabama. Drilling started both ends. Charles Ray collection. $75.00

3⅝" bannerstone preform found in Ohio. Charlie Wagers collection. $100.00

Notched ovate preform with pecked holes 6" long. Charlie Wagers collection. $150.00

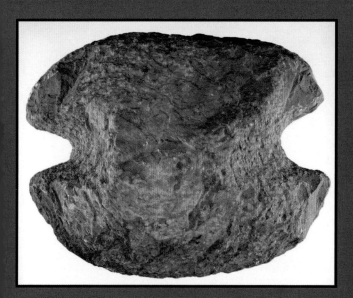

4¾" double notched preform made from slate. Charlie Wagers collection. $150.00

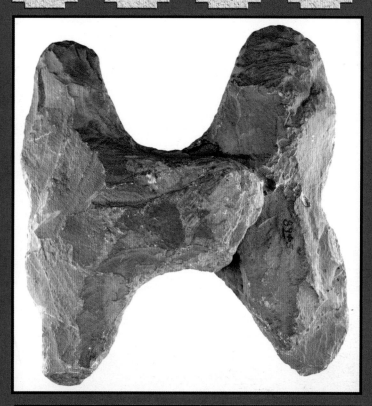

Double crescent preform made from slate. Charlie Wagers collection. $200.00

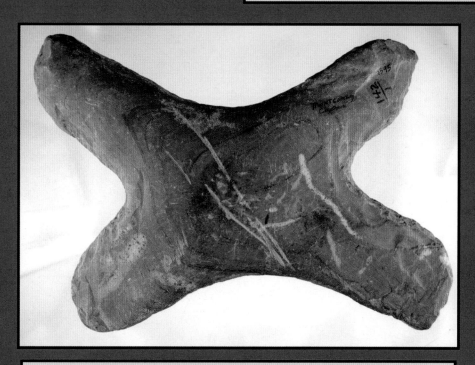

5⅛" double crescent preform. Charlie Wagers collection. $200.00

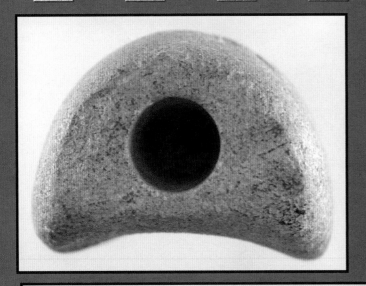

3" long x 1¼" thick saddleback banner preform made from granite. Found in Iredell Co., NC. Dennis Hess collection. $100.00

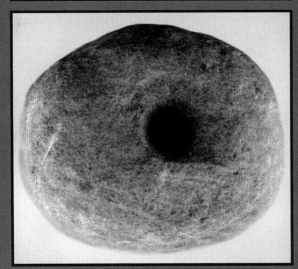

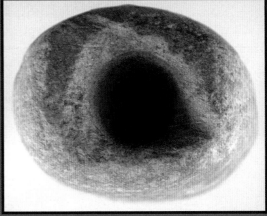

2¼" x 1⅝" banner preform found in Kentucky. Eric Wagner collection. $75.00

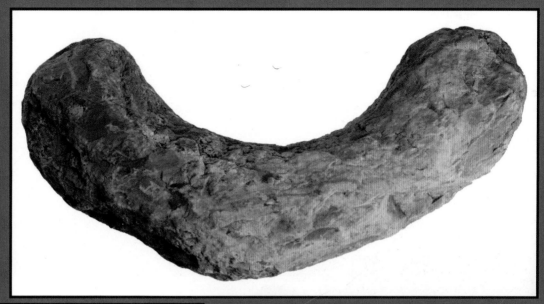

8" crescent bannerstone preform found north of Seamon Fort, Erie Co., Ohio. Ex. Vietzen. Gene Edwards collection. $75.00

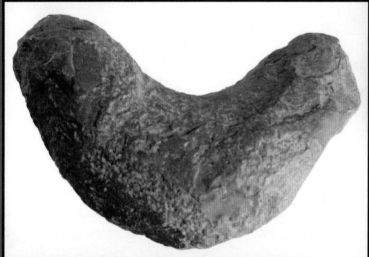

6¾" crescent bannerstone preform found in Nelson, OH. Ex. Vietzen. Gene Edwards collection. $50.00

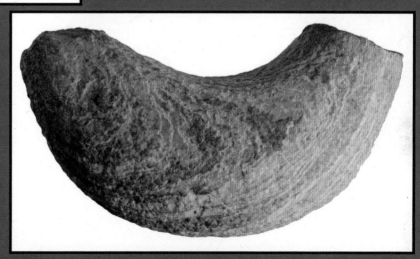

6½" crescent bannerstone preform found in Wabash City, IN. Gene Edwards collection. $50.00

7½" crescent bannerstone preform found in Etowah, TN. Gene Edwards collection. $125.00

7¼" crescent bannerstone preform. Gene Edwards collection. $200.00

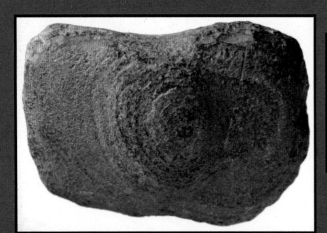

4¼" wing bannerstone preform. Gene Edwards collection. $30.00

7¾" wing bannerstone preform found three miles south of Columbus, west side of Scioto River in the summer of 1931. Gene Edwards collection. $50.00

6¾" wing bannerstone preform. Gene Edwards collection. $50.00

4¾" wing bannerstone preform. Ex. Viet- zen. Gene Edwards collection. $30.00

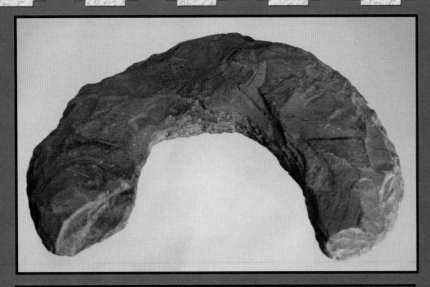

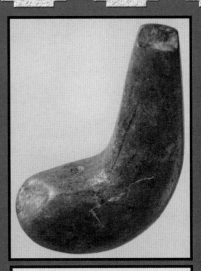

5¼" crescent preform. Gene Edwards collection. $60.00

3" geniculate preform with touch mark. Gene Edwards collection. $100.00

6" wing bannerstone preform. Gene Edwards collection. $150.00

4½" pick bannerstone preform. Gregory Edwards collection. $150.00

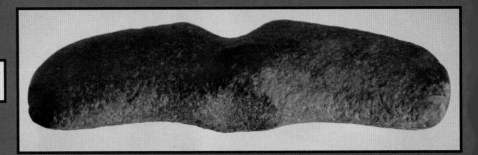

3½" pick preform found in Orange Twp., Ashland, OH. Gene Edwards collection. $125.00

3" wing bannerstone preform. Gene Edwards collection. $80.00

2½" wing bannerstone preform found in Sullivan Co., IN. Gene Edwards collection. $40.00

4" hardstone wing bannerstone preform. Gene Edwards collection. $50.00

7¾" wing bannerstone preform found in Point Pleasant, MI. Gene Edwards collection. $75.00

4¼" shield bannerstone preform found in New Jersey. Gene Edwards collection. $50.00

2½" bannerstone preform. Gene Edwards collection. $30.00

Bannerstone preform found in Kentucky. Gene Edwards collection. $80.00

2½" bannerstone preform found in Chippewa Lake, OH. Ex. Vietzen. Gene Edwards collection. $40.00

3¼" wing bannerstone preform found in New York. Gene Edwards collection. $50.00

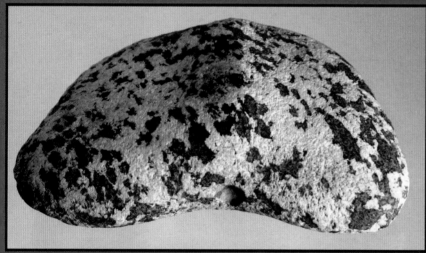

5" wing bannerstone preform found in Montgomery Co., OH. Gene Edwards collection. $50.00

6½" wing bannerstone preform. Gene Edwards collection. $50.00

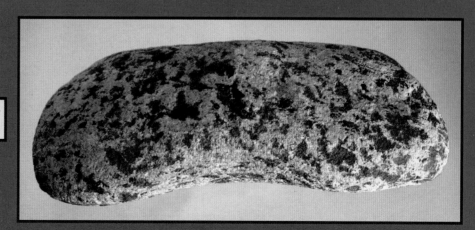

3" bannerstone preform found in Henderson Co., KY. Gene Edwards collection. $30.00

4¼" bannerstone preform. Ex. Vietzen. Gene Edwards collection. $80.00

2½" bannerstone preform. Gene Edwards collection. $50.00

3" bannerstone preform found in Allen Co., OH. Ex. Fred Fisher who bought it off finder. Gene Edwards collection. $50.00

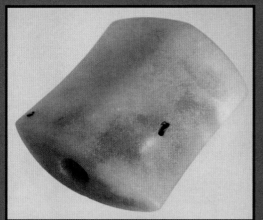

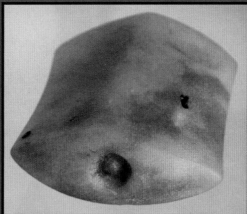

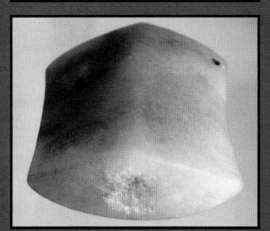

3" bannerstone preform found in Allen Co., OH. Ex. Fred Fisher who bought it off finder. Gene Edwards collection. $350.00

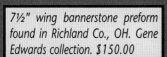

7½" wing bannerstone preform found in Richland Co., OH. Gene Edwards collection. $150.00

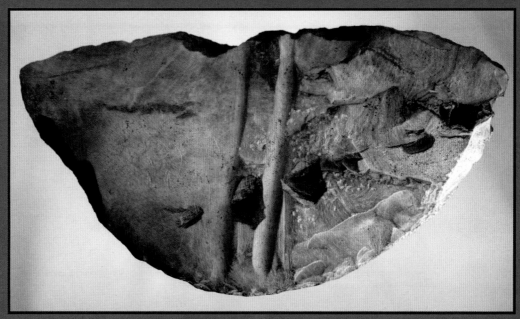

9" wing bannerstone preform found in New Jersey. Gene Edwards collection. $75.00

7¼" wing bannerstone preform found in Butler Co., Ohio. Gene Edwards collection. $50.00

7½" wing bannerstone preform found in Jefferson Co., IN. Gene Edwards collection. $75.00

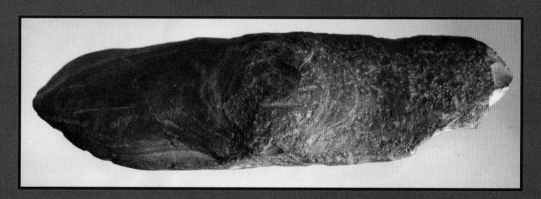

6¾" wing bannerstone preform. Gene Edwards collection. $40.00

6¼" wing bannerstone preform found in Tennessee. Ex. Fred Eisermore. Gene Edwards collection. $100.00

6" wing bannerstone preform. Gene Edwards collection. $100.00

6" wing bannerstone preform. Gene Edwards collection. $40.00

4½" wing bannerstone preform found in Ohio. Ex. Jim Snyder. Gene Edwards collection. $100.00

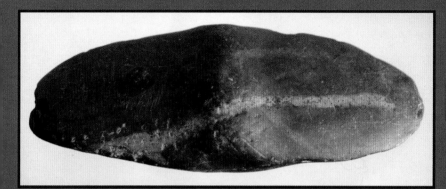

4" wing bannerstone preform found in Ross Co., OH. Gene Edwards collection. $125.00

6½" notched ovate preform found in southern Ohio near Ripley. Gene Edwards collection. $150.00

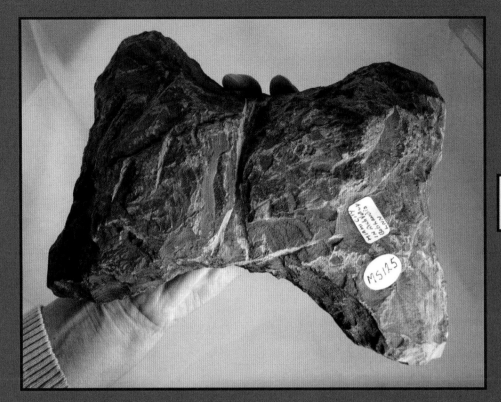

8" double crescent bannerstone preform found in Miami City in Rich Valley. Gene Edwards collection. $125.00

9¾" crescent bannerstone preform. Gene Edwards collection. $100.00

10" wing bannerstone preform found in Erie Co., OH, near Huron River. Gene Edwards collection. $125.00

8½" wing bannerstone preform. Gene Edwards collection. $125.00

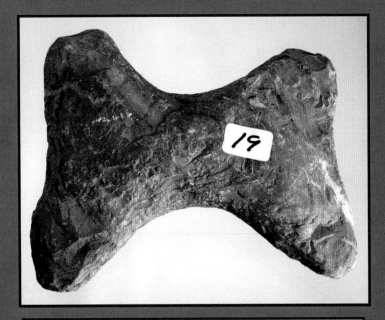

5¼" double crescent preform. Gene Edwards collection. $150.00

3" D-bannerstone preform. Gene Edwards collection. $60.00

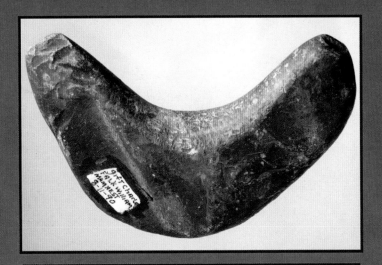

5¼" crescent bannerstone preform. Gene Edwards collection. $75.00

2½" bannerstone preform found in Miami Co., OH. Gene Edwards collection. $40.00

3½" bannerstone preform. Gene Edwards collection. $80.00

1¾" tube bannerstone found in Ohio. Gene Edwards collection. $100.00

8" crescent bannerstone preform. Gene Edwards collection. $120.00

1¾" quartz D-bannerstone preform found in Decator, AL. Gene Edwards collection. $30.00

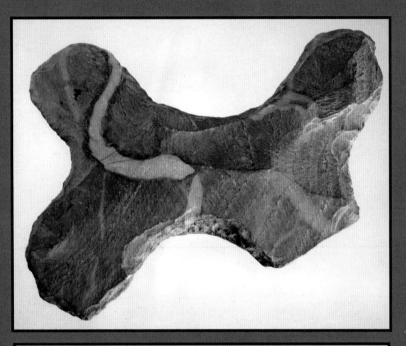

6" quadro concave preform. Gene Edwards collection. $150.00

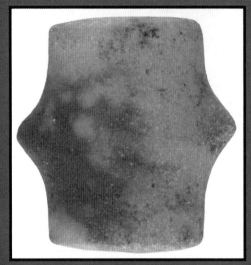

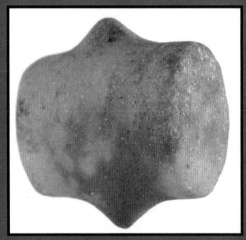

2¼" preform bottle bannerstone, quartz. Collection of Gary Noel. $850.00

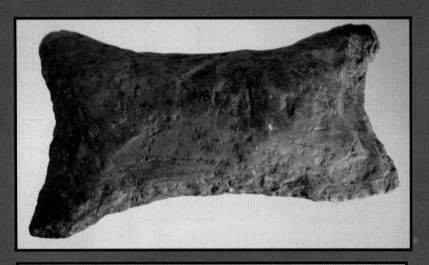

Double crescent preform. Gene Edwards collection. $150.00

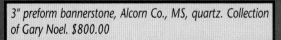

3" preform bannerstone, Alcorn Co., MS, quartz. Collection of Gary Noel. $800.00

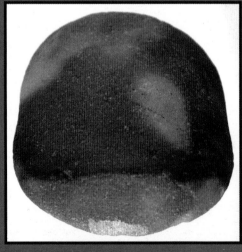

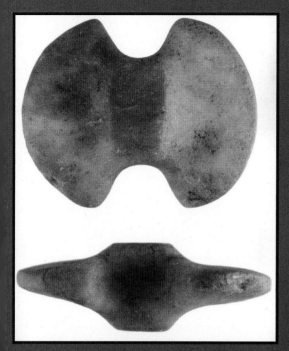

3⅜" preform winged bannerstone, quartz. Collection of Gary Noel. $1,200.00

6¼" blank slate pick bannerstone found in southeastern Illinois. Ex. Bingman. Lar Hothem collection. $75.00

5⅝" slate preform tube pipe or tube bannerstone. Found in Scioto Co., OH. Lar Hothem collection. $150.00

2⅞" granite preform bannerstone found in southeastern Illinois. Ex. Bingman. Lar Hothem collection. $50.00

3" partially drilled quartz bannerstone found in Posey Co., IN. Lar Hothem collection. $250.00

Gueiss preform, Ohio Co., KY. Jon Dickinson collection. $100.00

Banner preform. Personal find in southern Indiana on the Ohio River. Jon Dickinson collection. $50.00

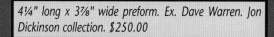

4¼" long x 3⅞" wide preform. Ex. Dave Warren. Jon Dickinson collection. $250.00

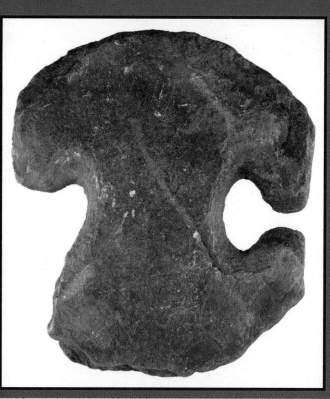

Since antler and bone decompose quickly in much of the Midwest, antler hooks are rare items. While photographing the collections that are represented in this book, I was lucky to come across some great examples of antler atl-atl hooks in two fantastic collections. I would like to thank the Museum of Native American Artifacts in Bentonville, Arkansas, for once again opening up their collection for study and photography, and I would also like to extend my appreciation to Mr. Charlie Wagers of Ohio for allowing me to visit, study, and photograph his exceptional collection of bannerstones and antler hooks.

5¹³⁄₁₆" antler atl-atl hook found in the Santa Fe River, FL. Exceptional example with dark river patina caused by tanic acid. Collection of Chris Smith. Museum Grade

2¹⁵⁄₁₆" long antler atl-atl hook found in Oklahoma. Ex. Edward Payne. Collection of Chris Smith. $800.00

1⁷⁄₁₆" long antler atl-atl hook found in Ohio. Collection of Chris Smith. Museum Grade

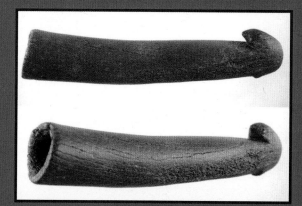

Atl-atl hook, 4½", river find in South Carolina. Charles Ray collection. Museum Grade

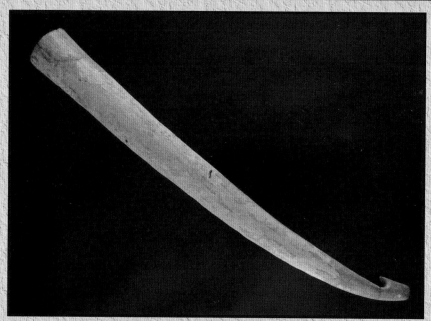

8" antler atl-atl hook found in Kentucky. Charlie Wagers collection. Museum Grade

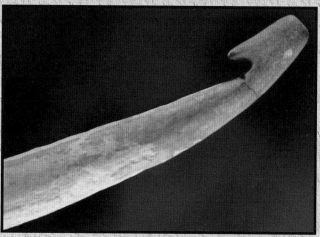

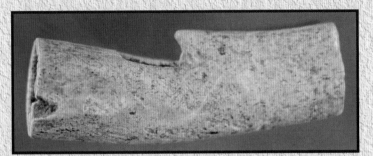

3½" antler hook found in Kentucky. Charles Wagers collection. Museum Grade

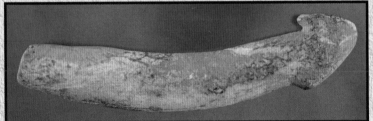

4⅝" antler hook, stylized. Charles Wagers collection. Museum Grade

7⅛" antler atl-atl hook found in Kentucky. Charlie Wagers collection. Museum Grade

4⅝" antler hook, stylized appreance. Found in Aucilla River, Taylor Co., FL. Charles Wagers collection. Museum Grade

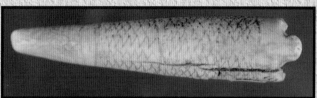

Rare engraved antler hook, 2⅞" long, found December 1959 in Watts Cave, Todd Co., KY. Charles Wagers collection. Museum Grade

Two 2⅞" and 5¾" antler hooks found in Aucilla River, Taylor Co., FL. Charles Wagers collection. Museum Grade

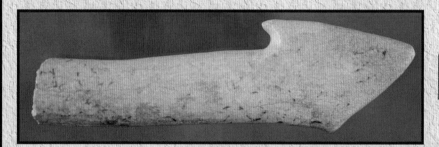

3¼" antler hook. Charles Wagers collection. Museum Grade

Group of damaged hooks. Charles Wagers collection. $100.00 – 300.00 each

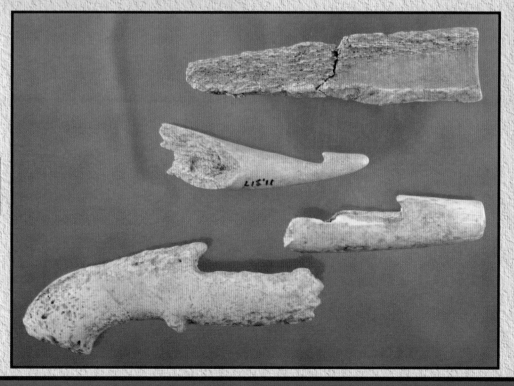

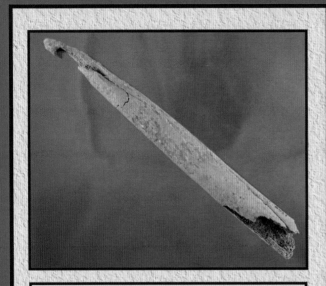

6¼" Kentucky hook that shows deterioration. Charles Wagers collection. $700.00

Alaskan ivory big hook, shows different style, but still an atl-atl component part. Charles Wagers collection. $1,800.00

Atl-atl hook found in Kentucky, 3½". Eric Wagner collection. $1,800.00

6⅜" atl-atl hook found in Arkansas and made from antler. Courtesy of the Museum of Native American Artifacts, Bentonville, AR. Museum Grade

6⅝" atl-atl hook. Courtesy of the Museum of Native American Artifacts, Bentonville, AR. $2,200.00

Atl-atl handle found in Kentucky and made from antler. Courtesy of the Museum of Native American Artifacts, Bentonville, AR. $350.00

Atl-atl handle found in Kentucky, made from antler. Courtesy of the Museum of Native American Artifacts, Bentonville, AR. $350.00

3¾" antler handle found in British Columbia along the Fraser River. Collection of Cliff Jackson. $350.00

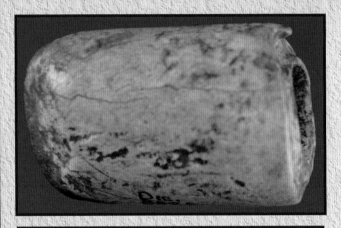

Hollowed bone cap style hook. This would have fit over the end of an atl-atl shaft. Sometime called a nubbin hook. Found by Hugh Dawsett in Dickerson cave in Todd Co., KY. 1⅝" long, 1" tall, made from Antler. Charlie Wagers collection. $350.00

Hollowed bone cap style hook. This would have fit over the end of an atl-atl shaft. Sometime called a nubbin hook. Found by Hugh Dawsett in Dickerson cave in Todd Co., KY. 1⅞" long, 1" tall, made from Antler. Charlie Wagers collection. $350.00

Antler hook, 2⅛", found in Arkansas. Charles Wagers collection. $350.00

Valuation Factors

Like any other artifact group, the value of an artifact hinges on many factors, some of those being:

Rarity of Style
Quality, Rarity & Appearance of Material
Condition
Size
Provenance
Appearance
Overall Desirability

Rarity of Style

Like all artifact groups, some specific styles were made in great quantity, and others in limited amounts, and that holds true for bannerstones. The actual number of specific types of artifacts created in ancient times depends on the length of time ancient man manufactured the items and the size of the geographic area in which it was manufactured and distributed. Basically, how many people were making the item and for how long? Bannerstones were limited in production to the Central U.S. with some east coast examples. Why the concept did not travel farther west with the trade routes that were established long ago, no one knows. When you have an item that was made in a small geographic area for a relatively short number of decades or centuries, you end up with rarity. Some bannerstones styles are more commonly available, while others are not often seen. With regard to rarity and price, it simply comes down to a matter of supply and demand.

Quality, Rarity & Appearance of Material

Was the bannerstone made from common gray slate, or beautiful rose quartz? Is it made from a plain hardstone or from beautiful speckled granite? Material quality is as important a factor when determining values as any of the other factors listed above. Plainly put, most all collectors will pay more for artifacts that display well and attract attention. Material plays a vital role in that aspect of collectiblity. If the bannerstone is made from a solid color gray, red, or black slate, it will not value as high as if it were made from green banded slate. If the green banded slate has beautiful and aesthetically pleasing swirled banding, it is worth even more.

Condition

No matter how high an artifact scores with all the factors, if it is damaged, it is not desirable to most collectors, and hence the value is greatly diminished. The amount of damage directly relates to the drop in optimal value, with a few small edge nicks being acceptable to many, while heavier damage can take what would have been a $1,000 banner quickly to the point of being a $50 study piece. The one type of damage that is most acceptable on bannerstones are "plow scars." Since the people who lived in the archaic period used shallow burial graves, many bannerstones have been turned up in the fields over the last 200 or so years, and many have come in contact with farming machinery. Often times, as the plow or disk comes in contact with the bannerstone, it will scratch the surface some as it pushes it out of the way. These are plow scars, and while they negatively affect the optimum value of the relic, they also positively increase the authenticity factor. If the plow scars are minor and do not affect the overall look of the item, the drop in value is not severe.

Size

Size is not as critical to a bannerstone as it is to many other artifact groups as most bannerstone types are fairly specific in the sizes they were made back in ancient times. With that being said, miniature bannerstones are quite collectible and will hold a higher value than a somewhat larger average sized banner. On the opposite end of the spectrum are the purely ceremonial styles which were intentionally made oversized and thus the large size increases the rarity factor which raises the value of the relic.

Provenance

With all of the modern reproductions that have flooded the market, bannerstones that can be documented back to the old-time collections bring a much higher value. If a banner was pictured in an older *Who's Who* book, or an older auction catalog, it is more likely believed to be authentic as it predates the modern con-artists. Keep in mind however, that reproductions have been made for well over 100 years. Having the documentation is great — but that does not make it authentic.

Appearance

The general appearance is a combination of all of the above factors, but adds in two other factors: symmetry, and finish. Is the bannerstone symmetrical in shape, well balanced, and even? Is the surface nicely polished on all areas? When you have a nicely balanced, well finished bannerstone made from a nice grade of material, you have a very collectible artifact that will bring a higher market value.

Overall Desirability

This factor changes depending on the part of the country you are in. I am in Ohio, so I find green banded slate more desirable than red claystone. My good friend John McCurdy lives in Mississippi and prefers the red colored claystone/siltstone to banded slate. I like winged banners, he likes "D" banners. The types, styles, and materials that come from a certain area will always be more collectible and more desired by those who live in that area. While some styles and material are in high demand in most all areas, others artifacts, bannerstones included, see vast regional differences in overall desirability.

Building a Bannerstone Collection

Bannerstones have been a much sought-after artifact type since collecting ancient Indian artifacts began. Beautiful in shape and form and often made from aesthetically pleasing material, bannerstones are not only a rare artifact type, but also very prone to breakage. Having a larger diameter hole than other slate artifact types, and with a distribution area that mostly resides in the freeze zones, moisture that accumulates in the dirt within the hole tends to freeze and expand, breaking the bannerstone in two. Finding a complete banner in the field while surface hunting is rare, and certainly a cherished find for any field walker lucky enough to come across a complete one.

Two collectors I came across while writing this book were lucky enough to find a complete bannerstone in recent years. Here are their stories:

Back on January third of 2006 I had planned on making a trip to Richmond, Kentucky, to an artifacts meeting. I woke up pretty early and decided to kill some time by doing a little hunting before making the five hour trip. At best I figured I may find a decent point to add to my display. A heavy thunderstorm the evening before made for great hunting conditions with moist soil and overcast skies. I started hunting the smallest knoll on this piece of land because I knew I could probably hunt a good portion of the site before I had to leave. This particular knoll doesn't usually give up many relics but the quality is usually above average for the area. On the second or third pass I spot a familiar shape in the soil. The very instant my eyes spotted the piece of slate I knew it was a notched ovate bannerstone. The big question was whether it was drilled. I took several photos from many different angles before picking it up. When I picked it up there was a clump of carpet weeds in one of the notches. I pulled on the clump of weeds and a perfect cylindrical plug of soil came out. In shock I immediately leave the field to print out my pictures for the meeting I would attend later that evening. I can't think of a better way to start a year than to find my first complete bannerstone as my first artifact for the year 2006.

Adam Agusti

I found the banerstone pictured here on December 22, 2007. I was hunting with a good friend of mine, Edward Stevens. We made a trip down to Coshocton County, Ohio, to check out some of the fields he used to hunt. We walked for about five hours with not much more than broken points to show for it. Ed said there was a farm that he hadn't hunted for many years, and he wasn't even sure if the farmer was still alive. It was late in the day, but after the day we were having anything sounded good, and you know it's hard to quit without finding something. As luck would have it the farmer was not only alive, but he was home too. He remembered Ed, and after about 45 minutes of chatting he told us we could hunt, but not to leave any trash in his fields. We thanked him and finally headed out. We walked the field directly behind his house with no better results than earlier in the day. We decided to drive over to the field on the opposite side of the farm. This field runs parallel to Wills Creek and had a nice terrace with lighter ground showing. I had a real good feeling when I saw that. We hit the field and I went straight to the ridge. Ed headed toward the lower section, and I went the opposite way. After about 20 minutes we were about 200 yards apart. I saw what I thought might the bit end of a banded slate celt sticking out of the ground. I had just pushed it a little with my walking stick when I saw the dirt plug in the hole. That's when my heart just about came out of my chest. Not knowing if it was whole or not I started yelling at the top of my voice for Ed to get over here. I didn't want to pull it out of the ground without him being there. He knew I had found something good because every time he started slowing down, I started yelling again. He actually covered the distance between us in pretty good time, but it wasn't fast enough for me. When he finally got over to me we both knelt down and I started pulling it out. I couldn't believe it when it came out and I got to see that it wasn't broken. Ed was as excited as I was, and it turned out to be a pretty good day. The banner is my best personal find to date, and I may never be lucky enough to find another. It is a great example, and a well used banner that must have seen many kills while it was attached to its atl-atl. I can only imagine the ancient hunter that made and used it.

Rob Dills

Since finding bannerstones is such a rare occurrence, most collectors turn to buying banners. As with all artifacts, the more desirable the relic type, the more reproductions one must wade through to find the authentic ones.

While certain more established artifact auction houses and online auction sites tend to always seem to have scores and scores of beautiful undamaged bannerstones available made from the finest materials in the rarest of styles, finding authentic documented examples with good solid history is not quite as easy a task. If you are new to collecting, it is important that you know Indian artifacts are reproduced in modern times at an astounding pace. Bannerstones being one of the more valuable types of artifacts automatically makes it a favorite of the reproduction con-artist.

One of my closest friends and business associates is a gentleman named John McCurdy who resides in Mississippi. I met John several years ago and what he was going through at the time reminded me of exactly what I went through over 20 years ago when I first began collecting. We both share the common bond of being burned on reproduction artifacts we thought were the real thing when we began collecting. This has happened to hundreds if not thousands of other new collectors.

The defining moment of whether a person continues to collect or decides to drop from the hobby altogether comes quickly after the realization that while you thought you were beginning to build a valuable artifact collection, in reality you only have in your possession an accumulation of worthless fakes. At that critical point, most people drop from the hobby. John however, like myself years ago, maintained his love of artifacts and the study of the ancient past, and has gone on to put together a wonderful collection of authentic artifacts.

One of John's favorite artifact groups to collect are bannerstones — predominately southern style banners. When I told John I was considering doing a page or so on reproductions and some of the pitfalls of collecting bannerstones, he related to me that he had kept every single reproduction he bought that first year he started collecting, and he would be glad to send me a photograph of them to use here. Knowing that John has since put together a quality collection of banners, I asked him to also send photos of his current collection to show newer collectors that between the pitfalls that are waiting out there for anyone trying to purchase artifacts, quality collections can still be assembled.

Collector John McCurdy with a selection of artifacts he bought in his first year that were represented as being authentic, but in fact were reproductions. John has kept all his reproduction as study tools and reminders that when buying artifacts, especially from auctions with no solid guarantees, you cannot be too careful.

John showing the selection of authentic artifacts he has assembled since that first year. All the artifacts pictured have multiple certificates of authenticity from the better known authenticators, and as you can see, John has developed a knack for seeking out quality flat slate and banners.

The John McCurdy Collection

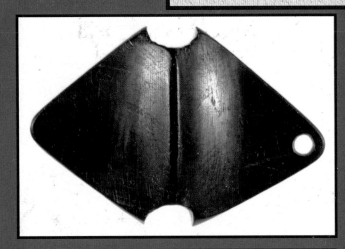

3⅛" double notched wing banner stone found in Clark Co., OH.

3⅝" bar amulet found in Portage Co., IN.

3¼" salvaged bar amulet found in Ohio.

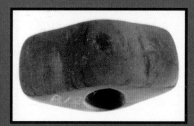

1⅝" miniature winged bannerstone found in Ohio.

2⁹⁄₁₆" miniature butterfly banner stone found in Ohio.

3½" tri-fluted tube bannerstone found in Ashland Co., OH.

3¾" panel banner stone found in Knox Co., OH.

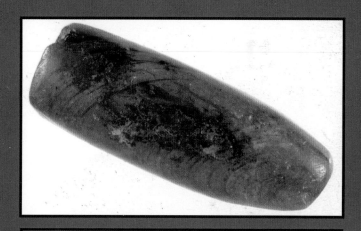

3¹¹⁄₁₆" tube bannerstone found in Portage Co., OH.

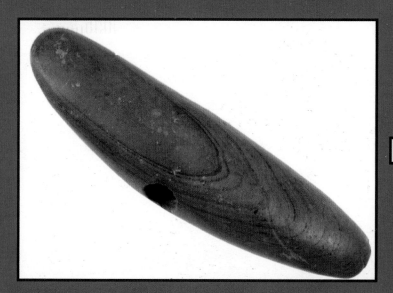

5³⁄₁₆" pick bannerstone found in Lorain Co., OH.

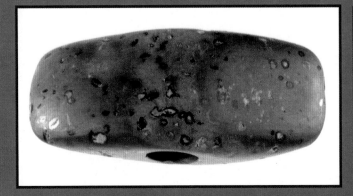

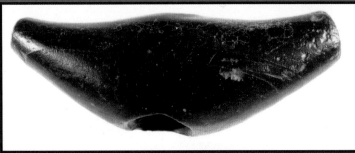

3⅝" pick bannerstone found in Hancock Co., OH.

3⁹⁄₁₆" winged bannerstone found in Allengan Co., MI.

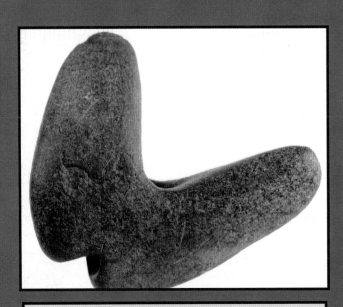

3½" cresent bannerstone.

3¾" rectangular tube bannerstone found in Hardin Co., TN.

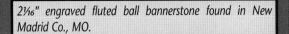

2¹⁄₁₆" engraved fluted ball bannerstone found in New Madrid Co., MO.

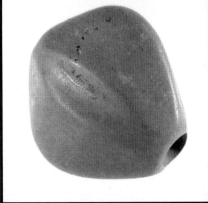

2¼" single faced bannerstone found in Clay Co., Arkansas.

2¼" winged bannerstone found in Georgia.

2³⁄₁₆" rectangular bannerstone found near Evansville, IN.

5⅞" winged bannerstone found in Erie Co., OH.

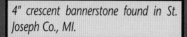

4" crescent bannerstone found in St. Joseph Co., MI.

3¼" geniculate bannerstone preform found in Summit Co., OH.

2" ridged bannerstone found in Richland Co., OH.

3¼" shuttle bannerstone found in Marion Co., MS.

2¾" shuttle bannerstone found in Obion Co., TN.

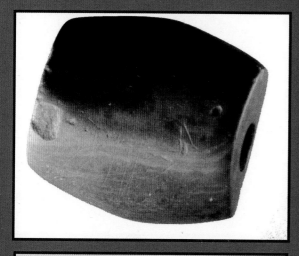

2¹⁄₁₆" bottle bannerstone found in Greene Co., AR.

2³⁄₁₆" unfinished shuttle bannerstone found in Alabama.

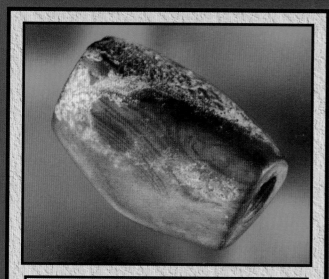

2¼" bottle bannerstone found in Vanderburgh Co., IN.

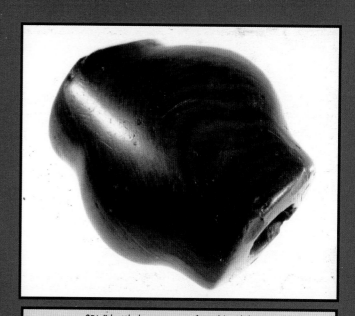

2⁷⁄₁₆" bottle bannerstone found in Alabama.

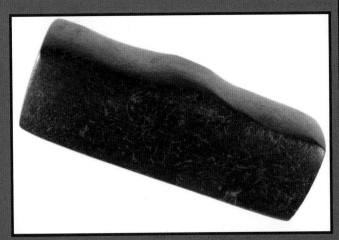

3⅞" Benton phase covered wagon bannerstone found in Alabama.

4⅛" reel bannerstone found in Colbert Co., AL.

4⅞" reel bannerstone found in Alabama.

1⅝" double edged bannerstone found in Autauga Co., AL.

2⅛" D bannerstone found in Cross Co., AR.

2" D bannerstone found in Aberdeen, MS.

2⁹⁄₁₆" D-humped bannerstone found in Jackson Co., IN.

2⁷⁄₁₆" humped bannerstone found near New Madrid, MO.

3⁵⁄₁₆" humped bannerstone found in Daviess Co., KY.

2⁵⁄₈" saddleback bannerstone found in Ohio.

4½" double edge winged bannerstone found in Tennessee.

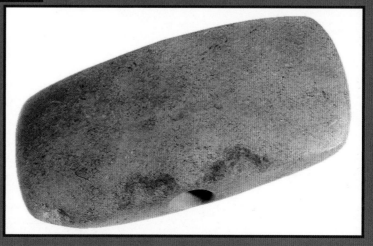

2" rectangular banner preform found in Yalobusha Co., MS.

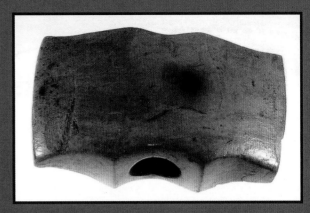

2⅝" shuttle bannerstone found in Yalobusha Co., MS.

1¹¹⁄₁₆" rectangular banner preform found in Yalobusha Co., MS.

3⅛" fluted tube bannerstone found in Kentucky.

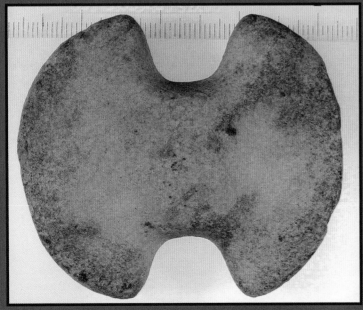

4" butterfly banner preform found in Yalobusha Co., MS.

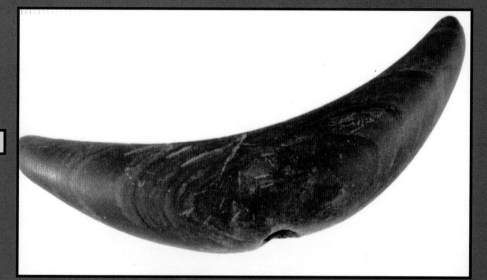

6½" lunate crescent bannerstone found in Ohio.

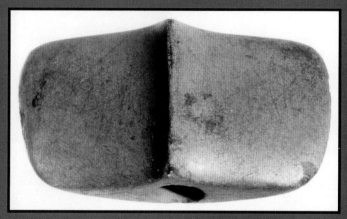

3⅝" winged bannerstone found in Arkansas.

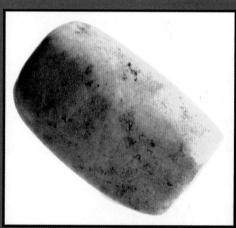

2½" Clarksville bannerstone found in Crawford Co., IN.

2½" D bannerstone found in Tennessee.

1⅞" D bannerstone found in Posey Co., IN.

3⁷⁄₁₆" shuttle bannerstone found in Savannah, TN.

3½" bannerstone found Hancock Co., IN.

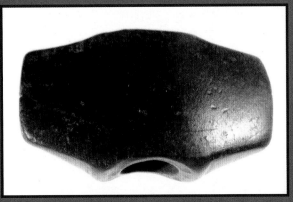

2⁹⁄₁₆" Benton phase winged banner stone found in Alabama.

1⁹⁄₁₆" miniature tube bannerstone found in Mississippi.

2½" saddleback bannerstone found in Harrison Co., IN.

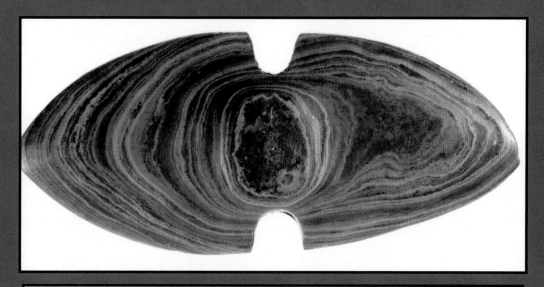

5⅜" double notched butterfly bannerstone found in Ohio.

7¼" lunate cresent bannerstone found in Hancock Co., IN.

Museum Quality Bannerstones

While there are many collectors who will obtain a bannerstone occasionally for their collection, only a handful specialize in seeking out the best-of-the-best bannerstones. While more than the few people featured here have put together quality bannerstone collections, I was lucky enough to receive invites from these gentle-men to photograph some of their truly museum quality bannerstones for this featured section.

All of the artifacts pictured in this section are muse-um grade, and prices on such items are determined strictly by weighing the desire to buy with the desire to sell, and thus no estimated value have been listed.

The David & Aaron Kilander Collection
Indiana

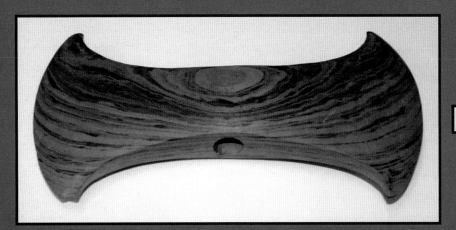

Double bit bannerstone, 6½", found in Illinois.

Winged bannerstone, 7½", found in Logan Co. KY.

Knobbed lunate, 7¹⁄₁₆", found in Williams Co. OH.

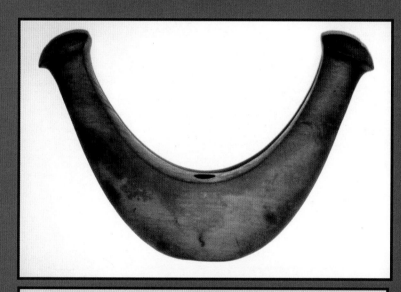

Knobbed lunate, 6¼", found in Jasper Co., IN. Ex. Bob Nesius collection.

Winged bannerstone, 6⅜", found in the Midwest.

Knobbed lunate, 8¾", found in Ashland Co., Ohio.

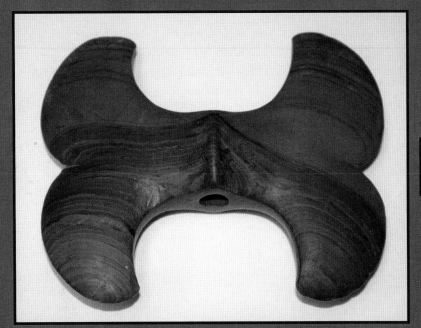

5" wide x 4⅛" tall. Ex. Townsend pictured in Mooreheads Stone Implements Vol. 1, page 393, Stone Ornaments, page 125.

Found in Rush Co., IN. Central States Journal #1. Ex. Townsend.

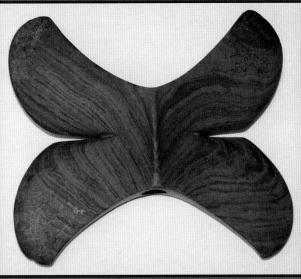

Winged bannerstone, 5½", found in Ohio.

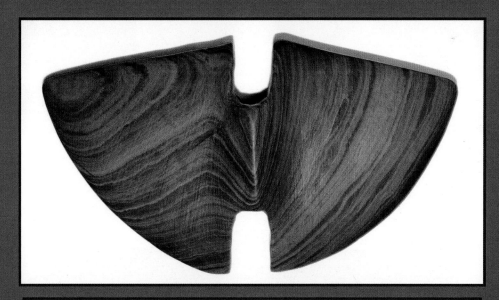

Notched winged bannerstone, 4⅝". Ex. Payne collection.

The Charlie Wagers Collection
Ohio

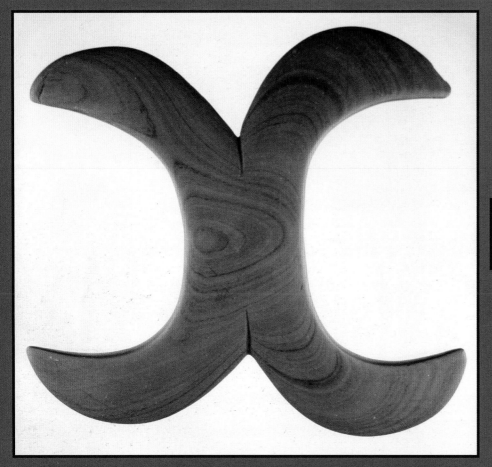

Double crescent, 6" x 6", found in Williams Co., OH. Ex. Leslie Hills, Edward Payne, Glen Groves, Byron Knoblock, Dr. T. Hugh Young, Clem Caldwell.

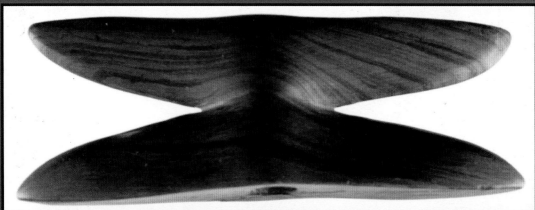

Reel bannerstone, 5⅝", found in Wilson Co., TN. Ex. E.L. Renno, Byron Knoblock, Dr. T. Hugh Young, Clem Caldwell.

Double notch butterfly bannerstone, 4" x 5¾", found in St. Joseph Co., IN. Ex. Sprague Chambers, Dr. Leon Cramer, Dr. T. Hugh Young, Clem Caldwell, Charlie Wagers.

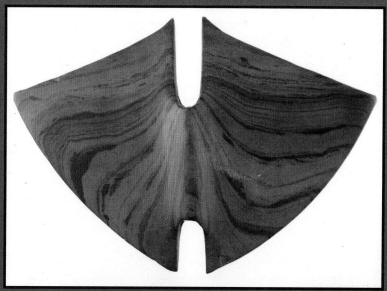

Notched ovate, 4½", found in Richland Co., OH. Ex. Jack Hook who bought from finder. Pictured in Ohio Slate Types.

Knobbed lunate, 5⅜", found in Trumble Co., OH. Ex. B. W. Stephens, Dr. T. Hugh Young, Clem Caldwell, Charlie Wagers.

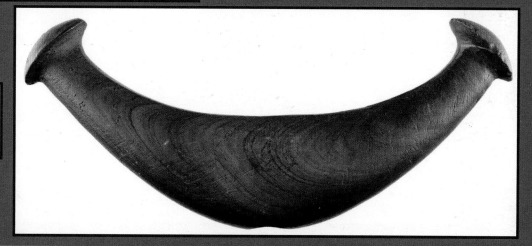

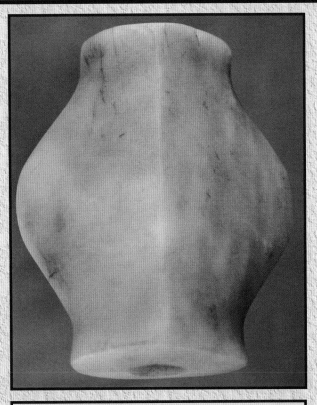

Quartz bottle bannerstone, 3¹⁄₁₆", found in Perry Co., MO. Ex. E. L. Renno, Dr. Prentis Chaney, Byron Knoblock, Dr. T. Hugh Young, Julian Gentry, Clem Caldwell.

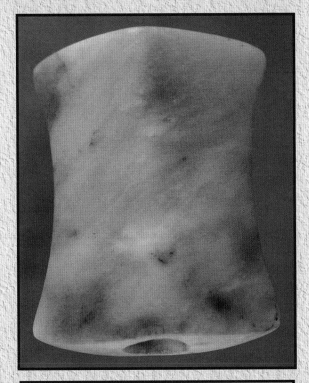

Hourglass quartz bannerstone, 2¹⁵⁄₁₆", found in Randolph Co., IL. Ex. Dr. P. F. Titterington, Dr. Prentis Chaney, Byron Knoblock, Dr. T. Hugh Young, Julian Gentry, Clem Caldwell, Charlie Wagers.

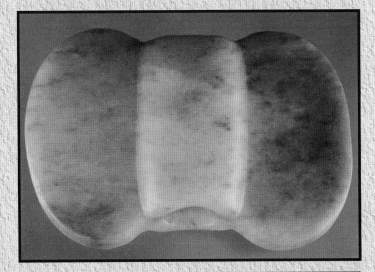

Quartz butterfly bannerstone, 2¾", found in Jersey Co., IL. Ex. B. W. Stephens, Dr. Hugh Young, Julian Gentry, Charlie Wagers.

Quartz bottle bannerstone, 1¾" x 1⅞", found in Boyle Co., KY. Ex. Lewis Bryant, Clem Caldwell, Charlie Wagers.

Green quartz saddle bannerstones, 2⅝" and 2⅝", found together in a child's grave in Kramer Mound, Spencer Co., IN, by Danny Glover. Ex. Art Gerber collection.

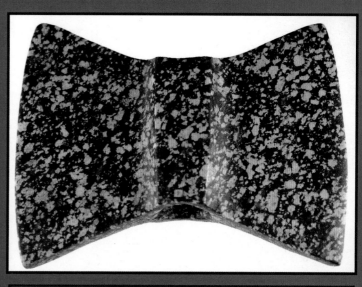

Wisconsin winged bannerstone, hardstone, found near Quincy, IL. Ex. B. W. Stephens, Dr. Hugh Young, Clem Caldwell, Charlie Wagers.

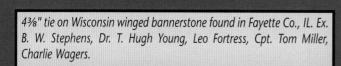

4⅜" tie on Wisconsin winged bannerstone found in Fayette Co., IL. Ex. B. W. Stephens, Dr. T. Hugh Young, Leo Fortress, Cpt. Tom Miller, Charlie Wagers.

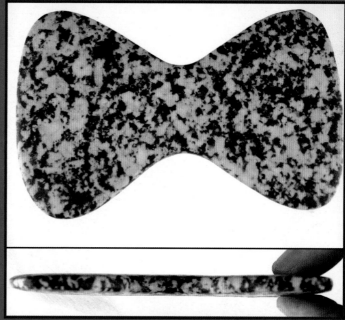

Pick bannerstone, chlorite material, 5³⁄₁₆", found in Madison Co., KY. Ex. Col. Bennett, H. Young, Raymond Vietzen, Charlie Wagers.

The Jim Crawford Collection
Missouri

Hourglass bannerstone, hardstone, 3¾" x 2⅛", found in Alabama.

2¼" x 1⅞" green banded slate ball bannerstone found in Union Co., IL.

4" x 2⁷⁄₁₆" granite winged bannerstone found in Wisconsin.

Fluted pick bannerstone, green slate, 5⅛" x 1⅜", found in Butler Co., OH.

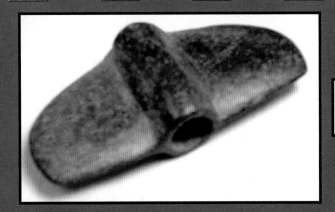

Whaletail bannerstone, 3⅜" x 1½", green seatite, found in North Carolina.

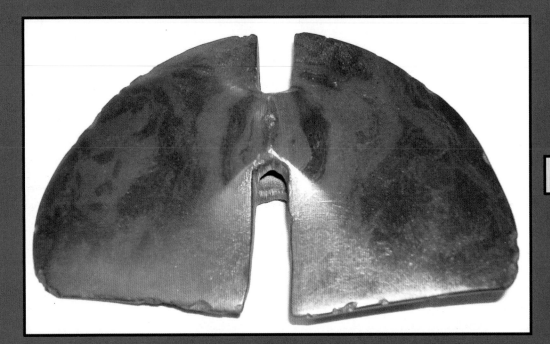

Butterfly winged bannerstone found in Mercer Co., OH, 5¹¹⁄₁₆" x 3¹⁵⁄₁₆".

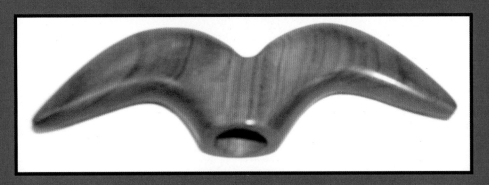

4¹⁵⁄₁₆" x 1½" crescent slate found in Indiana.

3¾" x 2⅝", found in Hancock Co., IN.

2⅝" x 2⅛" quartz butterfly bannerstone found in St. Clair Co., IL.

5¼" x 3⅛" winged bannerstone, notched butterfly. Found in Huron Co., OH.

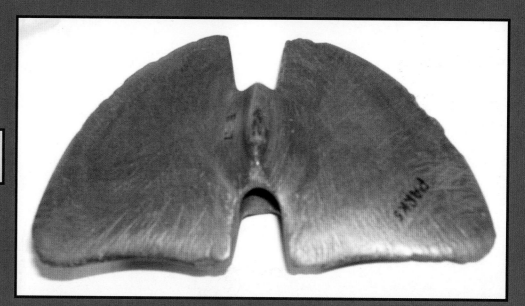

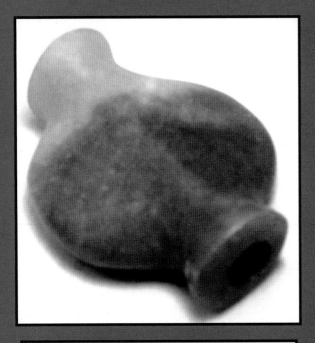

3¹⁄₁₆" x 2⅜" bottle bannerstone, quartz, found in Randolph Co., AR.

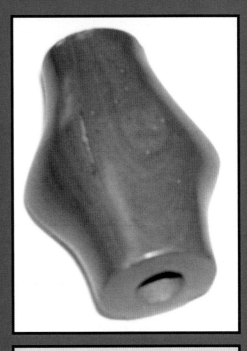

3⅛" x 2¼" red claystone bottle bannerstone found in Dunklin Co., MO.

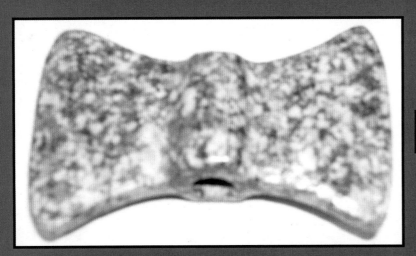

Wisconsin winged bannerstone, 3½" x 2¼", granite, found in Warrick Co., IN.

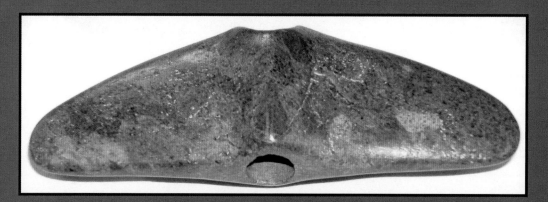

Whaletail bannerstone, serpintine phoryry, 5½" x 1¹⁵⁄₁₆", found in Greene Co., VA.

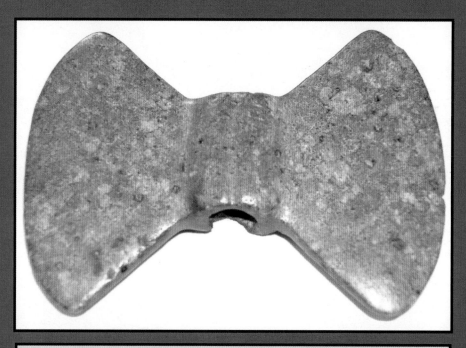

Wisconsin winged bannerstone, granite, 5¼" x 3¾", found in Page Co., IA.

Pick bannerstone, 4¹¹⁄₁₆" x 1⅜", red banded slate, found in Logan Co., OH.

2¾" x 2⅞" saddleback bannerstone found in Adams Co., IL.

3¼" x 2½" quartz bottle bannerstone found in Dunklin Co., MO.

5" x 1¾" crescent wing bannerstone, granite, found in Grant Co., WI.

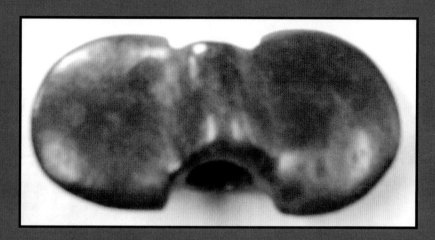

3¼" x 1⅝" butterfly bannerstone, mottled red claystone, found in New Madrid Co., MO.

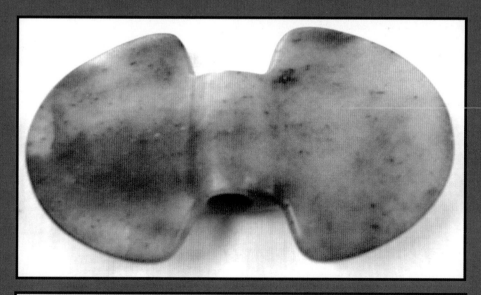

4⁹⁄₁₆" x 2⁹⁄₁₆" butterfly bannerstone, quartz, found in Warren Co., KY. Ex. Smail, LaDassor, B. W. Stephens.

The Tom Davis Collection
Kentucky

3⅝" x 2⅛" winged bannerstone found in Perry Co., TN.

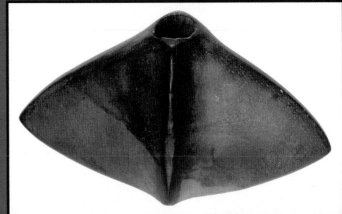

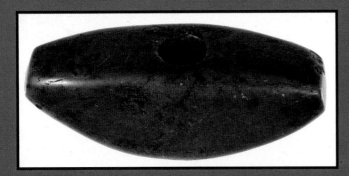

3⅜" x 1⅛" bannerstone made from Ohio pipestone. Ex. Ron Helman.

2½" x 2¾" bannerstone found in Stewart Co., TN.

2⅞" x 1⅞" saddle bannerstone found in Ashtabula Co., OH. Ex. Townsend, 1398.

4³⁄₁₆" x 1¼" Adena bar amulet found in Bath Co., KY.

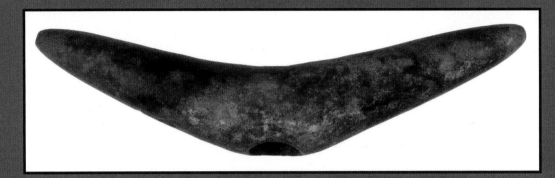

6⅛" long pick bannerstone found in Tennessee.

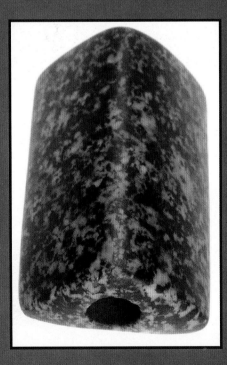

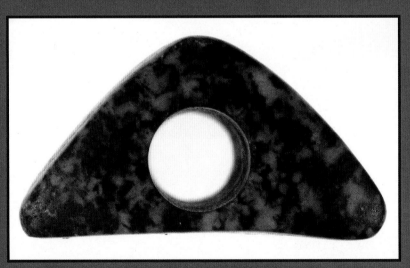

3¹⁄₁₆" x 2" saddle bannerstone found in Indiana.

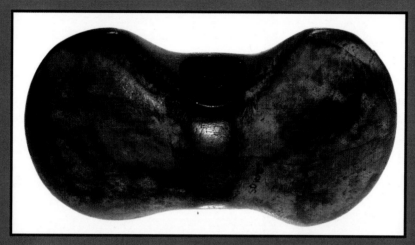

3⁹⁄₁₆" x 2⅜" butterfly bannerstone found in Kentucky.

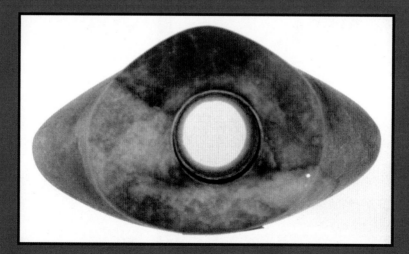

3¹⁄₁₆" x 2½" quartz bottle banner found in Illnois.

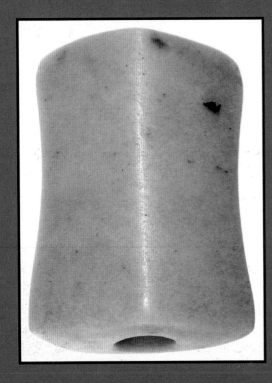

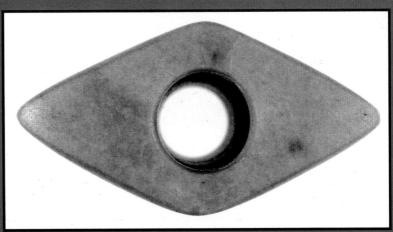

2¾" x 2" quartz bannerstone found in Davies Co., KY.

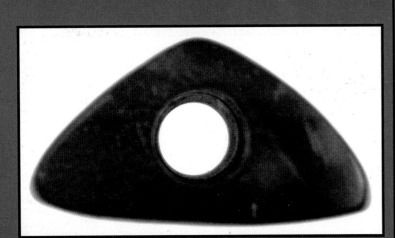

2⁷⁄₁₆" x 2⅛" saddleback bannerstone found in Tennessee.

3¾" long pick bannerstone found in Ohio.

4½" x 1⅝" bannerstone found in Ohio.

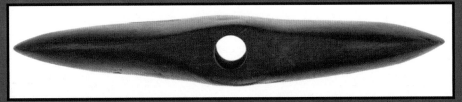

4⅞" x 2½" winged bannerstone found in Ohio.

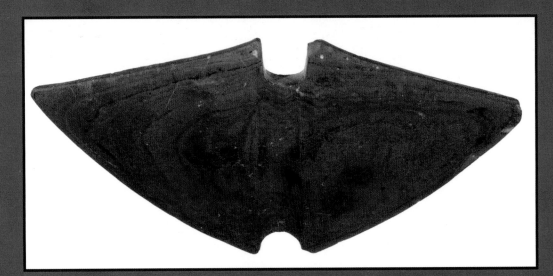

5⅝" x 3⅛" x ¼" thick tie-on winged bannerstone found in Ohio.

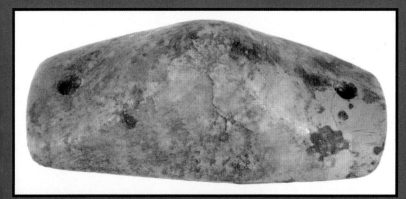

2½" x 1⅛" Galena boatstone found in Clark Co., KY.

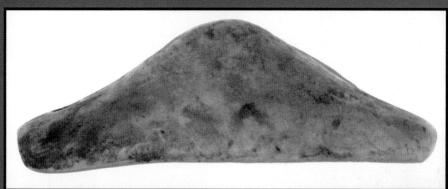

3½" x 1³⁄₁₆" Galena boatstone found in Clark Co., KY.

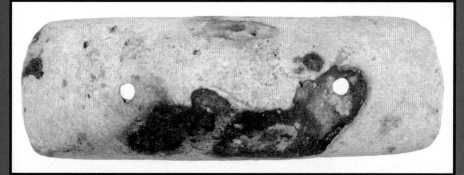

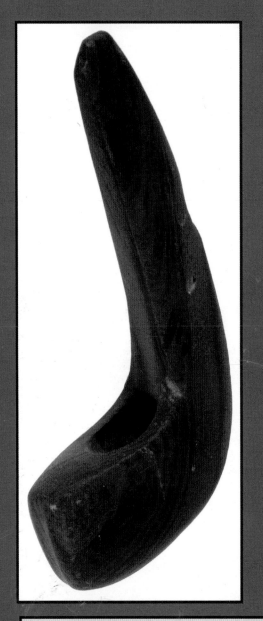
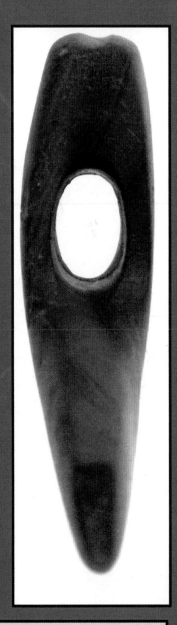

4⅜" x 2½" geniculate found in Cumberland Co., KY, near the Cumberland River in the mid 1700s. Ex. Richard Armstrong.

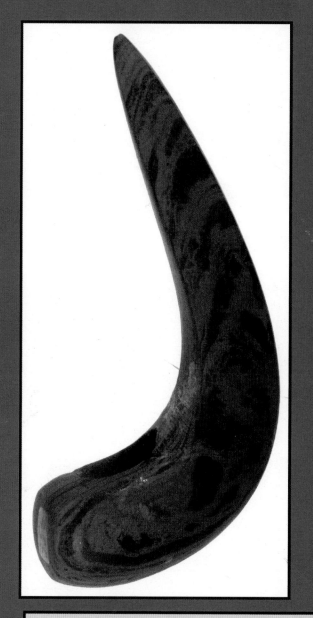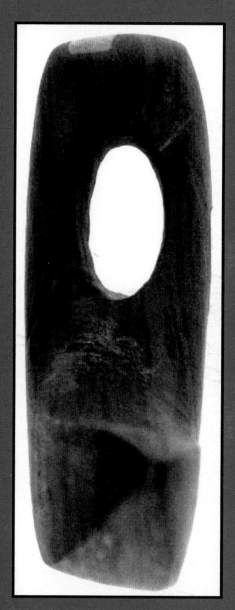

4⅛" x 2⅛" geniculate.

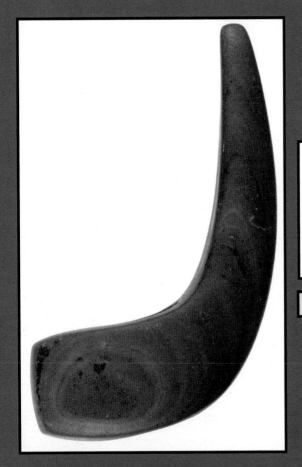

4¼" geniculate found in Albany, KY, in 1988.

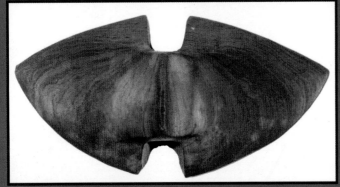

3⅞" x 1⅞" winged banenrstone found in Ohio. Pictured in Ohio Slate Types.

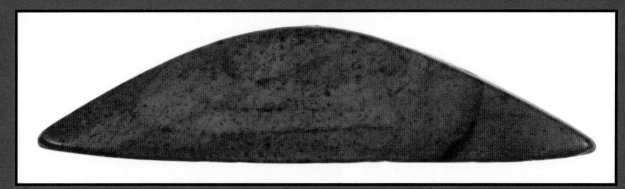

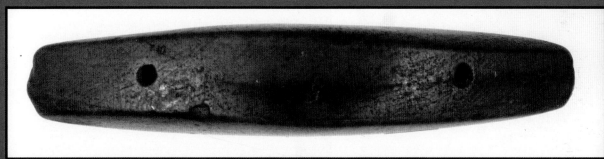

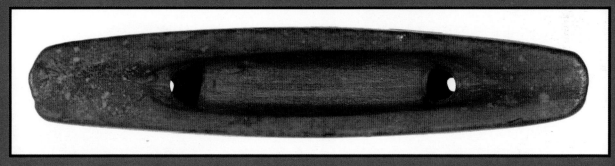

5¹⁄₁₆" x 1⅛" x 1" wide quartz boatstone found in Tennesse. Ex. Townsend.

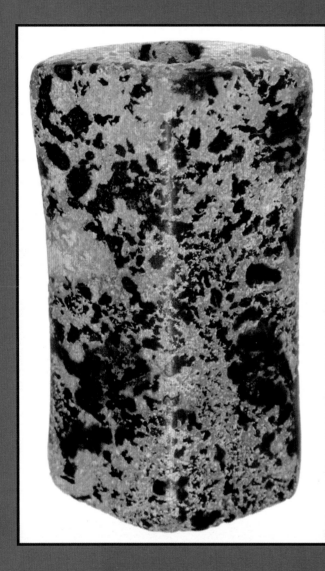

3½" x 2" prismoidal bannerstone found in Indiana.

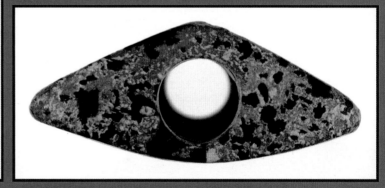

7½" long knobbed lunate found in Ohio by Thomas DeJarnette in 1924.

4⅝" x 2⅜" winged bannerstone found in Ohio.

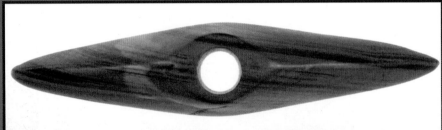

See caption at the bottom of page 201.

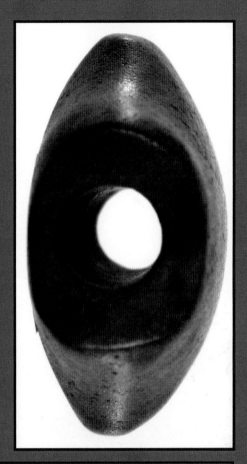

3⅜" x 2¼" hourglass bannerstone found in Henry Co., TN. Ex. Frank Morast.

3½" x 2¾" prismoidal bannerstone found in Indiana. Ex. Townsend.

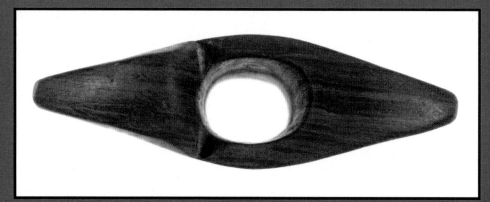

3" x 2⁷⁄₁₆" salvaged clipped wing bannerstone found in Ohio that is listed in the Lutz book and may be the rarest of all bannerstone types. It has an elongated hole as seen in panel banners and geniculates.

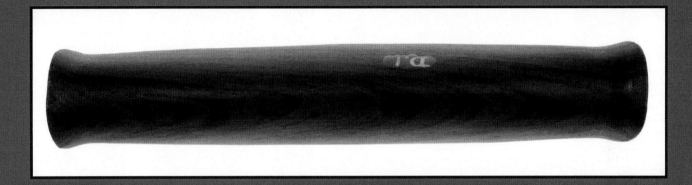

5⅜" x 1³⁄₁₆" amulet found in Hancock Co., IN. Ex. Meuser #900/5.

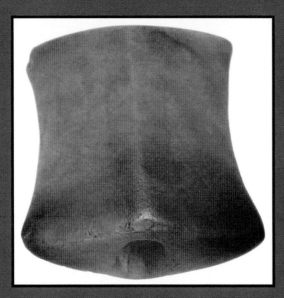

2⅝" x 2¼" rose quartz bannerstone found in Peoria, IL.

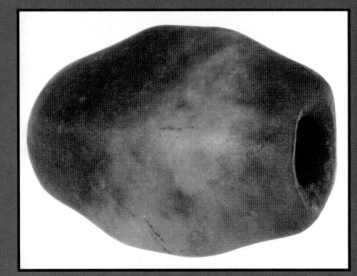

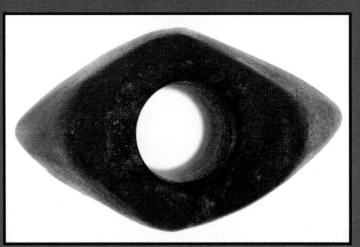

2⅞" x 2" hourglass bannerstone made from quartz, found in Kane Co., IL. Ex. C. Miles.

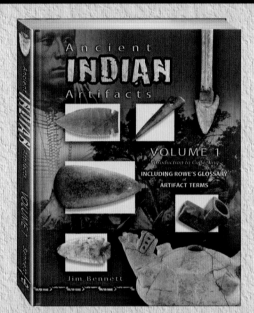

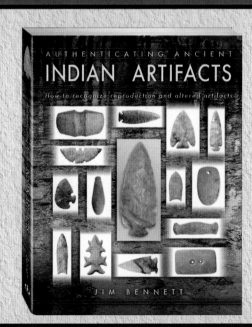

7534	Lancaster Glass Company, 1908–1937, Zastowney	$29.95
7359	**L.E. Smith Glass Company**, Felt	$29.95
6133	**Mt. Washington Art Glass**, Sisk	$49.95
6566	Standard Encyclopedia of **Opalescent Glass**, 5th Ed., Edwards/Carwile	$29.95
7364	Standard Encyclopedia of **Pressed Glass**, 5th Ed., Edwards/Carwile	$29.95
6476	**Westmoreland Glass**, The Popular Years, 1940–1985, Kovar	$29.95

POTTERY

6922	**American Art Pottery**, 2nd Edition, Sigafoose	$24.95
6326	Collectible **Cups & Saucers**, Book III, Harran	$24.95
6331	Collecting **Head Vases**, Barron	$24.95
6943	Collecting **Royal Copley**, Devine	$19.95
6621	Collector's Encyclopedia of **American Dinnerware**, 2nd Ed., Cunningham	$29.95
5034	Collector's Encyclopedia of **California Pottery**, 2nd Ed., Chipman	$24.95
6629	Collector's Encyclopedia of **Fiesta**, 10th Ed., Huxford	$24.95
1276	Collector's Encyclopedia of **Hull Pottery**, Roberts	$19.95
6637	Collector's Encyclopedia of **Made in Japan Ceramics**, First Ed., White	$24.95
5841	Collector's Encyclopedia of **Roseville Pottery**, Vol. 1, Huxford/Nickel	$24.95
5842	Collector's Encyclopedia of **Roseville Pottery**, Vol. 2, Huxford/Nickel	$24.95
6634	Collector's Ultimate Ency. of **Hull Pottery**, Volume 1, Roberts	$29.95
7530	Decorative **Plates**, Harran	$29.95
7638	Encyclopedia of Universal Potteries, Chorey	$29.95
7628	English China Patterns & Pieces, Gaston	$29.95
5918	Florences' Big Book of **Salt & Pepper Shakers**	$24.95
6320	Gaston's **Blue Willow**, 3rd Edition	$19.95
6630	Gaston's **Flow Blue China**, The Comprehensive Guide	$29.95
7021	Hansons' American **Art Pottery** Collection	$29.95
7032	**Head Vases**, 2nd Edition, Cole	$24.95
2379	Lehner's Ency. of **U.S. Marks** on Pottery, Porcelain & China, no values	$24.95
4722	**McCoy Pottery** Collector's Reference & Value Guide, Hanson/Nissen	$19.95
5913	**McCoy Pottery**, Volume III, Hanson/Nissen	$24.95
6835	**Meissen** Porcelain, Harran	$29.95
7536	The Official **Precious Moments®** Collector's Guide to **Figurines**, 3rd Ed., Bomm	$19.95
6335	Pictorial Guide to **Pottery & Porcelain Marks**, Lage, No values	$29.95
1440	**Red Wing Stoneware**, DePasquale/Peck/Peterson	$9.95

6838	**R.S. Prussia** & More, McCaslin	$29.95
7637	**RumRill Pottery**, The Ohio Years, 1938–1942, Fisher	$29.95
7043	**Uhl Pottery**, 2nd Edition, Feldmeyer/Holtzman	$16.95
6828	The Ultimate Collector's Encyclopedia of **Cookie Jars**, Roerig	$29.95
6640	Van Patten's ABC's of Collecting **Nippon Porcelain**	$29.95

OTHER COLLECTIBLES

7627	Antique and Collectible Dictionary, Reed, No values	$24.95
6446	Antique & Contemporary **Advertising Memorabilia**, 2nd Edition, Summers	$29.95
6935	Antique **Golf Collectibles**, Georgiady	$29.95
1880	Antique **Iron**, McNerney	$9.95
7024	**B.J. Summers' Guide to Coca-Cola**, 6th Edition	$29.95
1128	**Bottle** Pricing Guide, 3rd Ed., Cleveland	$7.95
7532	Bud Hastin's Avon Collector's Encyclopedia, 18th Edition	$29.95
6342	Collectible **Soda Pop** Memorabilia, Summers	$24.95
6625	Collector's Encyclopedia of **Bookends**, Kuritzky/De Costa	$29.95
7365	Collector's Guide to Antique Radios, 7th Edition, Slusser/Radio Daze	$24.95
7023	The Complete Guide to Vintage Children's Records, Muldavin	$24.95
6928	Early **American Furniture**, Obbard	$19.95
7042	The Ency. of Early American & Antique **Sewing Machines**, 3rd Ed., Bays	$29.95
7031	**Fishing Lure** Collectibles, An Ency. of the Early Years, Murphy/Edmisten	$29.95
7629	**Flea Market Trader**, 17th Edition	$15.95
6458	**Fountain Pens**, Past & Present, 2nd Edition, Erano	$24.95
7631	**Garage Sale** & Flea Market Annual, 16th Edition	$19.95
3906	**Heywood-Wakefield** Modern Furniture, Rouland	$18.95
7033	Hot **Kitchen & Home** Collectibles of the 30s, 40s, and 50s, Zweig	$24.95
7038	The Marketplace Guide to **Oak Furniture**, 2nd Edition, Blundell	$29.95
6939	Modern Collectible **Tins**, 2nd Edition, McPherson	$24.95
6564	Modern **Fishing Lure** Collectibles, Volume 3, Lewis	$24.95
6832	Modern **Fishing Lure** Collectibles, Volume 4, Lewis	$24.95
7349	Modern **Fishing Lure** Collectibles, Volume 5, Lewis	$29.95
6322	Pictorial Guide to **Christmas Ornaments** & Collectibles, Johnson	$29.95
6038	**Sewing Tools** & Trinkets, Volume 2, Thompson	$24.95
5007	**Silverplated Flatware**, Revised 4th Edition, Hagan	$18.95
7537	Summers' Pocket Guide to **Coca-Cola**, 6th Edition	$14.95

This is only a partial listing of the books on antiques that are available from Collector Books. All books are well illustrated and contain current values. Most of these books are available from your local bookseller, antique dealer, or public library. If you are unable to locate certain titles in your area, you may order by mail from COLLECTOR BOOKS, P.O. Box 3009, Paducah, KY 42002-3009. Customers with Visa, MasterCard, or Discover may place orders by fax, by phone, or online. Add $6.00 postage for the first book ordered and 70¢ for each additional book. Include item number, title, and price when ordering. Allow 14 to 21 days for delivery.

News for Collectors	Request a Catalog	Meet the Authors	Find Newest Releases	Calendar of Events	Special Sale Items

www.collectorbooks.com

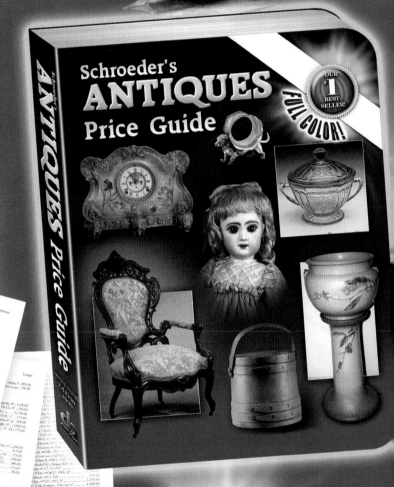